# Have a Nice Guilt Trip

# Have a Nice Guilt Trip

## Lisa Scottoline

AND

## Francesca Serritella

ST. MARTIN'S PRESS ✦ NEW YORK

HAVE A NICE GUILT TRIP. Copyright © 2014 by Smart Blonde, LLC, and Francesca Scottoline Serritella. All rights reserved. Printed in the United States of America. For information, address St. Martin's Press, 175 Fifth Avenue, New York, N.Y. 10010.

www.stmartins.com

Library of Congress Cataloging-in-Publication Data

Scottoline, Lisa.
  Have a nice guilt trip / Lisa Scottoline, Francesca Serritella. — First edition.
    pages cm
  ISBN 978-0-312-64009-5 (hardcover)
  ISBN 978-1-4668-3456-9 (e-book)
  1. Mothers and daughters—Humor.  2. Women—Humor.  3. Serritella, Francesca Scottoline.  4. Scottoline, Lisa.  I. Serritella, Francesca Scottoline.  II. Title.
  PN6231.M68S373 2014
  818'.5402—dc23

                                                              2014008566

St. Martin's Press books may be purchased for educational, business, or promotional use. For information on bulk purchases, please contact Macmillan Corporate and Premium Sales Department at 1-800-221-7945, extension 5442, or write specialmarkets@macmillan.com.

First Edition: July 2014

10  9  8  7  6  5  4  3  2  1

With all our love to Mother Mary

# Contents

---

# Introduction

---

By Lisa

Nobody knows more about guilt than women.

Especially this woman.

I don't have the time or space to list all of the things I feel guilty about, and I even feel guilty about that.

So I'll narrow it down and name only the things that I feel guilty about since dinner:

I feel guilty that I ate second helpings of rigatoni.

I feel guilty that I used tomato sauce from a jar.

I feel guilty that I didn't wash out the jar completely before I put it in recycling.

I feel guilty that I ran the dishwasher when it wasn't completely full.

Also, did I mention that Daughter Francesca is home visiting, and I feel especially guilty that I served my only child such a crappy dinner?

There is no guilt like Mom Guilt.

We are always failing our children in some way, aren't we?

At least I am.

Start with the fact that my daughter is an Only Child. I didn't give her any siblings, and that was because I divorced her father, whom I call Thing One.

Divorce Guilt.

I even divorced her stepfather, Thing Two.

Double Divorce Guilt!

(But don't worry, I bought her a lot of stuff to make up for it.)

Bottom line, if you're a mom, you'll feel guilty all the time, and this is true because you're a daughter as well, and God only knows how many times you failed your poor mother.

Shame on you, and guilt, too.

Now, to come to my point. If you think I'm going to preach to you that guilt is a bad thing, you're wrong.

I don't want you to change.

Because I like you just the way you are.

Don't lose your guilt. Embrace it, like me.

I don't feel guilty for feeling guilty.

I've long ago accepted that guilt is a part of me, like cellulite.

Guilt makes me work harder, do more errands, and get to the dry cleaners before closing.

Guilt means I'm always early, everywhere.

Guilt makes me pay my bills on time.

Guilt makes me nicer to people.

Guilt helps me be a better mother.

Guilt gets me on the elliptical. Occasionally, but only on Level One.

Guilt makes the journey of life into one long guilt trip. But in a nice way.

Hence the title of this book, *Have a Nice Guilt Trip*.

Herein you'll find true and funny stories from Daughter Francesca and me about life, both together and apart, since at twenty-seven years old, she has not only moved out, but stopped nursing.

We'll also tell a few silly and/or poignant tales about my mother, Mother Mary, who travels with a backscratcher and an attitude.

My guess is that our family will remind you of your family, except we're less well behaved.

So read on, and join us for the trip.

And come as you are.

# Homely Remedies

---

By Lisa

I hate it when Mother Mary is right, which is always.

We begin a zillion years ago, when I'm a little kid with a bad cold, and Mother Mary goes instantly for the Vicks VapoRub. As a child, I had more Vicks Vapo rubbed on me than most consumptives. My chest was as shiny as a stripper's and even more fragrant.

Camphor is still my favorite perfume.

Which could be why I'm single.

Another favorite home remedy of hers was the do-it-yourself humidifier. By this I mean she placed a Pyrex baking dish full of water on every radiator in the house.

I never knew why, and neither did my friends. None of them had radiators, because they had nicer houses. They had something called forced air, which sounded vaguely scary to us. The Flying Scottolines never forced anything, especially something you needed to breathe.

And in the summer, those same people had central air, which was something else we didn't have. Our air lacked centralization. The only central thing in our house was Mother Mary, and that was how she liked it.

But back to the do-it-yourself humidifiers, which sat like an open-air fishbowl on every radiator. As a child, I understood that this would cure something dreadful called Dry Air, which we had in spades. I didn't really understand why Uncle Mikey had to move to Arizona for the Dry Air, when he could've just moved to our house, but be that as it may, I was grateful that I had an all-knowing mother, who understood that air came in forced, central, and dry, and that everything could be cured by Pyrex.

The only time this was a problem was on Sundays, when Mother Mary actually wanted to bake ziti or eggplant parm, and there were no dishes available except for the ones cooking water on the radiators. She would dispatch me to get a Pyrex dish off the radiator and wash it out, and I would do so happily, if the end result was eggplant parm.

I will still do anything for eggplant parm.

Make a note, should we meet.

But back to the story, cleaning the baking dishes was a yucky job. Often the water in the dishes would have dried up, leaving a scummy residue, and even if there was some water left, it wasn't a pretty sight. Dog and cat hair would be floating on the surface, or ash from a passing cigarette.

According to Mother Mary, smoking was fine for air quality.

You win some, you lose some.

So fast-forward to when I become a mother myself, and baby Francesca gets sick, and of course Mother Mary advocates Vicks and Pyrex, but I reject these ideas as old-fashioned. I am Modern.

Enter antibiotics.

I had that kid so pumped up with amoxicillin she could've grown mold. In fact, I had her on them prophylactically, so she'd never get another ear infection, and if I could have her on them now, I would, so she'd never get pregnant.

I'm kidding.

It's a joke, okay?

But then recently, I got the worst cold ever, and I called the doctor, who told me that antibiotics weren't such a hot idea and what I really needed was Vicks VapoRub and a humidifier. I couldn't believe my ears. I wanted the magic pill to make it all better but he says that it's a virus and all that, and no.

I didn't tell this to Mother Mary. Don't you, either.

I suppose I could just get a Pyrex dish and put it on the radiator, but I am still Modern and I refuse. Also the doctor says I need a cool-mist humidifier, and not a warm-mist humidifier, and once again, I feel lucky to learn more about the mysteries of air, which now comes in mist.

Who knew oxygen could be so complicated?

So I go to the drugstore, buy the requisite cool-mist humidifier, and bring it home. I spend exactly one night with this thing and want to shoot myself. It's thirty degrees outside, and in my bedroom, it's twenty. An Arctic chill blasts from the cool-mist humidifier, and I'm up all night.

So I go back to the drugstore and buy a warm-mist humidifier. I take it home, and it frizzes my hair, but you can't have everything. Also, it comes with a little slot for a stick that's impregnated with Vicks VapoRub, and you know what I'm thinking.

This is the revenge of Mother Mary.

# Shades of Gray

---

## By Lisa

What's the difference between accepting yourself and giving up?

I'm talking, of course, about going gray.

Because that's what's happening.

I've had glimmers of gray hair before, but it was concentrated on the right and left sides of my head, which gave me a nice Bride-of-Frankenstein look.

But I've been working so hard over the winter that I haven't bothered to get my hair highlighted, and today I noticed that there's a lot more gray than there used to be.

And you know what?

It doesn't look terrible.

Also the world did not come to an end.

In fact, nothing happened, one way or the other.

But before we start talking about going gray, we have to talk about going brown. I seem to remember that brown is my natural hair color, but I forget. In any event, sometime in the Jurassic, I started highlighting my hair. It was long enough ago that highlights didn't require a second mortgage.

But no matter, some women are vain enough to pay anything to look good, and she would be me. I figured my highlights were a cost of doing business. In fact, I named my company Smart Blonde, so highlights were practically a job requirement, if not a uniform.

In fact, maybe highlights are deductible.

Just kidding, IRS.

(I know they'll really laugh at that one. They have a great sense of humor.)

Anyway, my hair appointment for new highlights is tomorrow, but I'm really wondering if it's worth it. Not because of the money, or even the time, but because I'm starting to accept the fact that my hair is not only secretly brown, it's secretly gray.

And so I'm thinking, maybe I should just let it go. Accept that I'm not only going gray, but I'm going brown, which I used to think was worse. And that maybe I should just accept myself as I am.

Or, in other words, give up.

Now, before I start getting nasty letters, let me just say that I love silvery gray hair on people. I know women who look terrific with all-over gray hair, but mine isn't all-over yet. It's coming only in patches, which looks like somebody spilled Clorox on my head.

You know you're in trouble when your hair matches your laundry.

Also, my gray hair is growing in stiff and oddly straight, so it looks like it's raising its hand.

But that might be my imagination.

And before you weigh in on this question, let me add the following:

I'm also deciding whether to start wearing my glasses, instead of contacts. Yes, if you check out the sparkly-eyed picture of me on the book, you'll see me in contacts. Actually, I took them out right after the photo, because they're annoying. Fast-forward to being middle-aged, where any time you're wearing your contacts, you have to wear your reading glasses, and so one way or the other, glasses are going to get you.

And I'm starting to think that's okay, too. In other words, I may be accepting myself for the myopic beastie that I am.

Which is good.

Or I may merely be getting so lazy that I cannot be bothered to look my best.

Which is not so good.

Because in addition to gray hair and nearsightedness, I also accept that I don't have the answers to many things. For example, I just drove home from NYC and I don't know the difference between the EZ-Pass lane and the Express EZ-Pass lane.

Life isn't always EZ.

# Baby Fever

---

By Francesca

Spring means one thing: babies.

My friend and I, plus my dog Pip, were enjoying an outdoor brunch at a restaurant and we were surrounded. Babies in sun-hats strapped into strollers, babies hanging their chubby limbs from their snugglies, babies gurgling on their parents' laps. The sidewalk was a baby parade. It was distracting.

But not as distracting as the words "vanilla buttermilk pancakes" on the menu.

My mouth had just begun to water when my friend cried out, "Omigod! Look at that munchkin!" She pointed to a baby in his mother's arms one table over.

"Cute," I said. I patted my lap once and Pip jumped into it. I taught him that, and it fills my heart with pride when he does it.

"You didn't even look."

"I looked." And I decided on the omelet.

"You don't feel that?" she asked.

"Feel what?"

"Baby fever."

I'm immune.

Later, when we were paying the check, my next-door neighbor approached, pushing her new baby in a stroller and walking her cockapoo. We greeted each other, and my friend cooed over her baby as I bent to pet the dog. When my neighbor left, my friend asked, "Is her baby a boy or a girl?"

I shrugged, feeding Pip some eggs from my plate, making sure to pick out the onions first. Onions aren't good for dogs.

"Do you know her baby's name?"

"Um . . . I know her dog's name is Jefferson."

"You're terrible!"

Am I?

Look, I'm not a monster. I like babies for all the obvious reasons. They're cute. They're soft. They have great laughs. And even when they throw food in a restaurant or cry next to me in an airplane, it never bothers me. I'm able to tune them out.

But is that bad?

Shouldn't there be some primitive part of my brain to prevent me from "tuning out" a child in need?

Even my dog Pip looks up when a puppy on a YouTube video gives a little yelp.

I'm counting on these maternal instincts to kick in down the road. But should there be more evidence of them now?

"I'm sure I'll feel the baby urge eventually," I said, suddenly unsure. I wiped some bits of egg Pip had gotten stuck in his ear fur. "We have time, don't we?"

"Sure, but I want one now."

I visibly shuddered.

I'm not prepared for a baby right now. I was an only child, I had no younger siblings, and my lone cousin is ten years older than I am. I have zero baby experience. I don't know how to hold, feed, or change a baby, and the mere thought of doing something wrong and breaking it gives me a cold sweat.

If I were a twenty-something man, this cluelessness would be understandable, even endearing, the stuff of rom-com movie montages.

As a woman, it's concerning.

"I wouldn't say it's 'concerning,' it's just surprising," my friend said, as we continued our discussion walking down the block after brunch. "You're one of the most nurturing people I know."

I do love to play mama to my friends. I bring soup to pals feeling sick, I text reminders for mutual friends' birthdays, I carried my BFF's passport for her when we studied abroad, and I enjoy surprising my boyfriend with freshly baked muffins in the morning.

But nurturing a twenty-five-year-old man is a lot different from nurturing an infant.

Well, at least they go potty on their own.

We stopped for Pip to do his business on the sidewalk. "I know I want kids someday." I paused to clean up after him. "I mean, I think I do."

My friend scrunched her nose in disgust.

"Sorry." I forget poop is gross.

The trash can was across the street behind a giant puddle. Pip couldn't jump it, so I scooped him up, cradled him in my arms, tossed the baggie, and walked back, still carrying him.

I felt desperate to defend my position to my friend as much as to myself. "Maybe I'll feel it when I'm more established in my career. Or maybe because of my parents' divorce, finding the right guy seems like the more challenging task, and I can't see past that yet. Or maybe"—I didn't even want to say the next thing aloud, it made me so sad—"maybe I'm not the baby type after all."

My friend was smiling at me. "Or maybe you just don't want another one."

Pip licked my chin.

Sweet baby.

# Fun for Free

---

By Lisa

Here's something I do that might be crazy:

I rearrange the furniture.

Often.

Blind people don't stand a chance in my house. And most of the time, neither do I.

Rearranging the furniture is one of my favorite bad habits. My most favorite bad habit is eating chocolate cake, and my least favorite bad habit is marrying badly.

It all began with an ottoman, which somehow expanded into the Ottoman Empire.

Let me explain.

I was sitting on my couch in the family room, working on my laptop with the TV on. I went to put my feet up on the coffee table, and my foot knocked over a mug of coffee. This had happened to me more times than I can count. Every book on my coffee table has been soaked with coffee, and so has the table itself, but I don't think that's why they call it a coffee table or a coffee-table book.

Right then and there, I decided to do something about it. I remembered that I had an ottoman in my office upstairs, which was paired with a chair that's there for show.

Please tell me I'm not the only person who has furniture for show.

The chair-and-ottoman sits next to my desk in case somebody wanders in, puts their feet up, and watches me work, but that's never going to happen and I wouldn't want that, anyway. Once I met a writer who told me that he read the pages he'd written that day to his wife, and I thought:

That poor woman.

In any event, I got the ottoman, carried it downstairs, plunked it down in the family room, and put my feet up on it.

Yay!

In the end, I ended up changing the fabric on the couch to coordinate with the ottoman and even changed the paint color on the walls, which is how the ottoman became the Ottoman Empire, and a bad habit was born.

Since then, I look around my house with a critical eye, wondering if the current furniture arrangement is the best and invariably deciding that it isn't. This thought usually strikes around bedtime, when all the smart people in the world would probably go to sleep.

But not me.

I shove couches around, then chairs. I even rearrange pictures on the wall and start hammering nails. Pick up any one of the framed things on my wall, and behind it you'll find at least twelve holes, like automatic-weapons fire, but really tiny.

Frankly, I don't think there's anything wrong with this bad habit.

On the contrary, I'm a fan. That's a great part of growing older, you start to think that even the bad things about you are good.

And why not?

Whose life is it anyway?

Rearranging the furniture is a way of having fun, for free. It keeps you on your toes to think about what other ways the room can be reconfigured, even if it means that you'll stub your toe on a chair that didn't used to be there.

In a funny way, I think it's a small-scale way to improve your own life.

Case in point is my alarm clock.

I know this sounds trivial, but why stop now. Somebody has to write about the simple things in life, and if you like that sort of thing, you've come to the right place.

I have this really large, ugly, glowing clock next to my bed, which I've suffered with for years. The numbers need to be big because I can't read them otherwise, and I need to know the time if I wake up at night, so I can worry about how much sleep I'm not getting.

I put things over the clock so it's dark enough to sleep, but it's not the best solution, to cover a clock with a pair of cotton undies, like the world's ugliest night-light.

Then it struck me that I could put the clock in the bathroom. Granted, I can't see it from the bed, but on account of my advanced years, I'm in the bathroom at least once a night.

And now I know exactly when.

Plus I sleep like a baby, and my cotton undies are back on my tushie.

Happy ending.

# With Apologies to Mary Poppins

By Lisa

My life just changed in a good way. In fact, in a great way.
By gummi vitamins.

I'm supposed to take a multivitamin, B complex, calcium,
CoQ10, and Crestor.

But the only thing I take is Crestor. Why? Because I don't like
taking pills, or I forget, and pills suck.

That would be a medical term.

So imagine my delight when I'm cruising the aisles in the
food store, and I see a massive jug of gummi vitamins. I don't
mean gummy, like my piecrust. I mean gummi, like the bears.

I get my gummi vitamins home and they're exciting and
colorful, shaped like blueberries, orange slices, and red cher-
ries. In other words, vitamins morphed into Jujyfruits.

I'm so there.

And I'm picking red goop out of my teeth as we speak.

There's a visual. Now you know why I'm dateless.

All of a sudden, I can't wait to take my daily multivitamins.
I'm like a little kid. They're better than Flintstone vitamins
because they don't stick together. Don't ask me how I know.

I get to have two gummi vitamins a day, and every morning, I look forward to picking my flavors. Never mind that

they all taste the same, like the first ingredient, which is Glucose Syrup.

It's candy with a medical excuse.

Sugar with a doctor's note.

A spoonful of gummi helps the medicine go down.

But it doesn't stop there.

I go back to the store, where they had Vitamin B Complex in gummi form, and they're awesome, too. Soft and chewy, in flavors that taste basically of floor wax.

But still.

Gummi!

And like a gummi addict, I went on another hunt and managed to find Gummi CoQ10 at Costco.

Don't ask me what CoQ10 is. It's not even a word. It's a password. It can't even make up its mind between numbers and letters. It should have to choose.

All I know is that my doctor said I have to take CoQ10 because I take Crestor, and he's the one man I obey.

Unfortunately my gummi CoQ10 is only peach-flavored, but that's still an improvement on CoQ10 in conventional pill form, which tastes like a conventional pill.

And it's a bitter pill to swallow.

So far, if you're counting, that means every day, I get to have five gummi things and call it medication. Which means that sugar, carbs, and calories don't count. And I'm not that crazy anyway. I actually love the taste of calories. In fact, calories are my favorite food.

Now you might be wondering about calcium, and that's where Viactiv comes in. Because I couldn't find gummi calcium, which would be the best thing ever. After gummi Crestor, which they have in Heaven.

But Viactiv calcium comes in chocolate and is wrapped in a square like a baby Chunky. So I grabbed those babies and started chowing down. By the way, Viactiv calcium also comes in caramel, raspberry, and chocolate mint. Yes, there are fifty-seven flavors of calcium, according to Dr. Baskin Robbins.

I did notice online that Viactiv now comes in chocolate vitamins, too, but they're no match for gummi vitamins, and I like a mixture in my meds, like Halloween candy.

They can't all be Snickers.

The only problem with chocolate calcium is that it's hard to limit yourself to forty-five servings.

I'm starting to think that all of our medical treats are compensation for being middle-aged and having to take all these dumb pills. In fact, whoever invented gummi medicine is a great person. Why shouldn't we get to have a little bit of fun with our cholesterol? Why can't we whoop it up while we make our bones stronger? And what's wrong with making a game out of whatever it is that CoQ10 does?

And think of the possibilities. If they made gummi birth-control pills, nobody would ever forget to take them.

And if they made gummi Viagra?

Run for cover.

# The Married-Ex Milestone

By Francesca

Your twenties are jam-packed with life's milestones—graduations, serious relationships, new jobs, major moves—and as Facebook notifies you when each of your friends makes any one of them, it's hard not to compare yourself and come up short.

A major milestone for me was actually the milestone of somebody else: when the first of my ex-boyfriends got married.

It was over a year ago now, just days before my twenty-sixth birthday. I had been cooped up during the homestretch of a book deadline and had been avoiding the distractions of the Internet. But on the very last day of editing, in a moment of weakness, I hopped on Facebook. In the first thirty seconds of looking at the home page, a new update appeared in the Newsfeed:

My college boyfriend was married.

It knocked the wind out of me. I instantly closed the Internet window but not fast enough to undo the knowledge. I didn't burst into tears, but I stood up from my desk, full of adrenaline with nowhere to go. Facebook only lets you *think* you know everything about everyone, and as my ex was never one to disclose his relationship status online, I didn't see this coming. No girlfriend, no engagement, just married. Just, all of a sudden, married.

Until then, I had felt like I was over the relationship; I'd had several relationships begin and end since ours. But he was the only boyfriend with whom I had ever discussed marriage. He was the only one I had fantasized about seeing at the end of the aisle.

And now he had already walked it, in real life, with somebody else.

My last relationship had ended almost a year ago, and I hadn't met anyone special since. Now even the most recent ex had a new girlfriend, and my college sweetheart had a wife.

Where did that leave me?

It sounds crazy, but I held a magazine up to cover the majority of the computer screen as I carefully navigated into my Facebook settings and blocked all future updates from my married ex. We had over a hundred mutual friends, and I didn't want to be inundated with all of the congratulations and "likes" on the news, or—oh God—the pictures.

Seeing your ex's wedding pictures is unnatural.

I did the remainder of my book edits in a daze, distracted by my complicated feelings. We had been off and on for a period of years. Through other relationships, I had always held a candle for him, and he for me. If you've read my writing before, you may recall that he was the one for whom I traveled across the country as part of a grand gesture to win him back.

It didn't work.

After everything, it was me who had put an end to the back-and-forth, the undefined in-between, because I knew it wasn't good for me. I needed a clean break.

And a year later, he was married.

Part of me was truly happy that the closure had worked for him. But had it worked for me?

I took account of my life. I was living in New York City, as I had always wanted to. I was working full-time as a writer, a dream I hadn't thought I'd get to pursue so soon. I had no right to complain.

But I wasn't in love.

I didn't even have a crush.

So I moped around my apartment, wearing sweats and listening to Adele's "Someone Like You" on repeat. On the third day, my friend Lucy emailed me. She invited me to see some band play that Friday and meet her boyfriend, the band's producer. I agreed, not so much because I wanted to go, but because I knew I needed to get out of the house.

I had reached the red zone of unwashed hair.

Getting ready on Friday night, I put extra effort into looking good in the hopes that I'd feel better about myself. My makeup felt like war paint, applied with a delicate brush. With my glumness hidden by a great blusher and some lip-gloss, I was ready for the night.

This was Sparta! Emotionally speaking.

It almost worked. My *tromp-l'œil* fabulousness fooled everyone but me. At preshow drinks with the girls, I felt a beat behind the happy conversation. All I really wanted to talk about was my ex, his startling elopement (or at least as I imagined it), his mystery wife (I mean, who *IS* this person?), and how lucky I was to have dodged that bullet, right?

RIGHT?!?

I knew these weren't winning conversation topics, so I kept my mouth shut and listened to the others gossip about how the band's drummer was so hot, but more trouble than he's worth.

Aren't they all?

We traipsed over to the music venue, with me lagging only a little behind. I was the last to reach the bouncer.

"You're beautiful," he said, handing back my ID with a smile. "Do me a favor. Don't get married tonight."

I looked at him like he might be clairvoyant. "Don't worry, I won't," I answered, meaning it.

At the show, I actually began to enjoy myself. There was a happy hubbub amongst the crowd, and my mind was kept busy with a whirlwind of introductions. When the band began setting up onstage, I saw one particularly handsome player. He had to be the jerk.

I elbowed my friend. "Is that the drummer?"

"No! That's the lead singer. It's his band. He's really nice."

*Yeah, right,* I thought bitterly. But I did edge my way around the crowd for a better view.

It turned out the lead singer really was nice. Three days after that night, he and I went on the best first date I've ever had, and he's been my boyfriend ever since. I'm not sure he's the one I'm going to marry, but I'm okay with not knowing. I'm okay with pretty much everything in my life right now, even if I am in between milestones.

This summer I went to my fifth-year college reunion. My ex wasn't there, but I heard that he and his wife recently had a baby. My first thought?

Nice, but I hope he didn't steal one of my awesome baby names. (He didn't.)

And that's when I knew: I was over my married ex.

How's that for a milestone?

# Brusha Brusha Brusha

---

By Lisa

So it turns out that dogs need more than love and food.

I learned this when I was talking to Francesca on the phone and she's brushing Pip's teeth, which she does every night. She also brushes his fur and trims his nails.

"Why don't you just let him be a dog?" I ask her, only half-kidding.

"Because I love him and I want to take care of him. You love your dogs, right?"

"Yes."

"So you need to take care of them. If you don't clip their toenails, it messes up their feet. Plus, Cavaliers have heart trouble, and tartar in their teeth only makes it worse."

I listen, intrigued. I remember my cardiologist saying it's good to floss your teeth because it keeps tartar from building up in your heart. After that, I never looked at tartar sauce the same way.

Francesca was saying, "I read that if you clean your dog's teeth, they can live one to three years longer. Wouldn't you want Peach to live three years longer?"

"Of course," I answer truthfully. I want Peach to live forever. Ruby, on the other hand, is a different story.

I'm allowed to have a doggie favorite. They don't know. And they won't tell their shrinks.

Francesca continues, "It's not that hard to clip their toenails, Mom. Just get one of those clippers with the hole. Don't cut the quick because it's a vein, and make brushing their teeth a game. Use peanut-butter toothpaste."

"I'm on it," I tell her, meaning it, but it takes me a month to buy the supplies and another month to give it a shot. It's a chore, when you have more than one dog. Four dogs times four paws equals a lot of toenails.

That would be the extent of my math ability.

Also I'm not sure I know how many toes a dog has, though I'm guessing it's five more than I want to clip.

I begin with Little Tony, the least disobedient of my disobedient dogs. The nail clipper looks oddly like a pair of pliers with a hole in the middle, and its package reads, Dog Guillotine Nail Trimmer.

This would be bad marketing.

Dog and guillotine don't belong in the same sentence.

Also it comes with a styptic pencil "to pack a quicked nail," and already I'm looking for a tourniquet.

I pick up the clippers, put Tony in my lap, and bring the clippers toward his curved black toe, which does look a little Fu Manchu. But as soon as Tony sees the clippers, he writhes back and forth. I can't get his nail in the hole.

The other dogs stand around laughing and pointing. The joke is on them because their nails don't look good.

Anyway, I try again and again to clip Tony's toenail, fighting the struggling dog, but I get so nervous I'm going to cut a doggie artery that my hand starts shaking.

I think immediately back to the days when Francesca was a baby and I had to clip her fingernails. I bought a pair of baby fingernail clippers, but she kept moving her hand around, fussing.

My own hand started shaking, thus guaranteeing that if I kept trying, I would amputate.

So I gave up, and when she was thirteen, she clipped her own nails.

But I digress.

I gave up on doggie toenail-clipping and segued into doggie tooth-brushing, but that didn't go well, either.

Dog toothpaste doesn't come with a toothbrush, but a weird plastic glove that has a rough patch on one finger.

And if you try to brush your dogs' teeth, you're in for a rough patch.

I follow the directions, which tell me to "introduce your dog to the toothpaste."

Dog, meet toothpaste. Toothpaste, meet dog. Everybody, meet woman with too much time on her hands.

So I open the toothpaste, which is green, gummy, and smells like pine trees. The box says it's peanut-butter flavor, but if I were a dog I would sue.

Guaranteed this is going to taste like Pine-Sol.

I sit on the rug with the glove and the toothpaste, and all four dogs edge away, then scoot out of the kitchen. I chase them around but they run under tables and chairs. I can't catch any of them except Penny, who clamps her mouth shut with the jaw pressure of a pit bull.

So I gave up.

Moral of the story? Sometimes it's okay to give up.

Works for fingernails and diets.

# Mother Mary and
# The Fighting Scottolines

By Lisa

We begin when Mother Mary falls seriously ill and has to be rushed to the hospital.

Don't worry, this will get funny by the end.

But in the middle, we learn that her legs are swelling, which is somehow connected to her heart. This I cannot explain, and even after a week with her in the hospital, I still don't understand. I thought the leg bone was connected to the hip bone, not the heart, but that's beside the point.

Mother Mary enters the hospital in Miami while I'm on book tour, and Brother Frank tells me it's serious, so of course, I cancel the end of the tour and fly down there with Daughter Francesca. I also asked my best friend and assistant, Laura, to come, which turned out to be essential because she served as referee.

It turns out that The Flying Scottolines cope with a life-threatening situation by threatening each other's lives.

The bad news is that Mother Mary was critically ill, in that her heart wasn't doing very well, functioning significantly under its capacity. The good news is that there are medications they put her on, blood thinners and the like, and to fast-forward so you all don't get upset, by the end of the week, she's stabilized and headed for cardiac rehab, with a good prognosis.

But the ones who need rehab are Brother Frank and me.

When the going gets critical, we get criticizing.

My brother and I normally get along very well, and I usually defer to Frank's judgment about what's good for Mother Mary, especially because they live together. But something about seeing my little mommy lying in bed, like an oddly gray-haired child, brings out the Hospital Nazi in me.

Or at least, I'm in no mood to compromise when her health is at stake.

And he feels the same way.

So we fight.

Over everything.

We spend all day at the hospital, and the scene is the same every day for almost a week: Francesca and Laura take care of Mother Mary while Frank and I fight.

What do we fight about?

Frank thinks she needs the top of her bed cranked up, but I think it's better lower. Frank thinks she needs her grippy socks on, but I think she doesn't. Frank thinks the window shades should be down, but I think they should be up. Frank wants the door open, but I want it closed. And don't get me started on the volume levels of the TV.

Obviously, we fight over the important things.

We fight in front of her, but then we realize that it upsets her, so then we take it out in the hallway, where she knows we're fighting but can't hear exactly why. At no point do we stop fighting. In other words, if she isn't having a heart attack, we're going to give her one. Because we love her so much.

Yes, we love her enough to kill her.

Now *that's* Italian.

Or maybe it isn't. Please tell me we're not the only family who behaves the worst when they should behave the best.

The only thing we agree on occurs on Day Five, when we

both agree that Mother Mary needs to be on oxygen. Unfortunately, Mother Mary doesn't think she needs oxygen to live.

So Frank and I, in a rare moment of unanimity, ask the doctors if she needs to be on oxygen, and they administer a test, which shows that oxygen is in order.

Peace reigns.

For a moment.

Because the decision about the oxygen starts Mother Mary fighting with Frank and me, thus triangulating our fists of fury.

Not only that, Mother Mary segues into taking a consensus of hospital personnel on the subject. She asks the next nurse to walk into the room: "Do I really need this oxygen?"

"Yes," answers the nurse.

A different nurse comes in, and Mother Mary asks her, "I think this oxygen is on too high. Will you check it, please?"

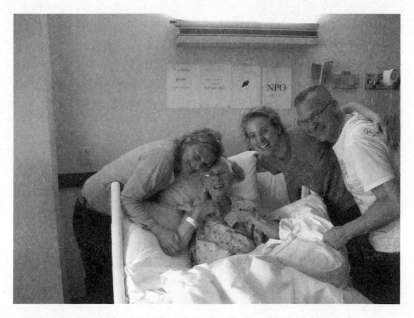

**A rare moment of solidarity by Mother Mary's bedside**

The nurse does and tells her, "That's the lowest it will go."

Then the orderly comes in for her lunch tray, and Mother Mary asks him, "How long do I have to be on oxygen?"

And he answers, "As long as the doctor ordered."

"Grrr," says Mother Mary.

Francesca and Laura go over to calm her down, and Frank and I exchange glances.

Mother Mary has only just begun to fight.

And we should know.

# Mother Mary Misbehaves

Mother Mary is out of the hospital, and recovery lies ahead. For the hospital.

Yes, Mother Mary is fine, and the hospital has almost recovered from her visit.

As you can imagine, she wasn't exactly the ideal patient. We've already discussed the fact that she didn't like the oxygen, and it won't come as news that she didn't like the food, the lighting, or the Kleenex, which was too small.

Evidently, she likes big Kleenex. The Flying Scottolines have supersized noses. A paper towel is a good start.

Please understand that I'm not criticizing her in her criticism of the hospital. I think I'd be grumpy, too, if you told me something was wrong with my heart. And way back when, you wouldn't want to have seen me in labor and delivery.

It was a labor to deliver me.

They monitored her blood pressure three times a day, but Francesca, Frank, Laura, and I monitored her grouchiness. We hoped her blood pressure went down, and her grouchiness went up. The unhappier she got, the happier we got. Mother Mary is at her healthiest when she's giving everybody else high blood pressure.

We knew she had turned a corner toward the end of the week, which was a big day. Her treatment was ending at the main hospital, but the question was whether she would be admitted to another hospital for cardiac rehab. One of the saints, also known as nurses, took us aside and said that she had to play better with others if she was going to graduate. So on the appointed day, we all sat her down in the principal's office.

Guess who was the principal.

Me.

"Ma," I said, "today, there are going to be two doctors who are going to interview you. You have to be nice."

"Why?"

"Because if they think you're an uncooperative patient, they won't let you into cardiac rehab."

"What do I care? I want to go home."

So you see what a bad principal I am.

And unfortunately, Mother Mary has aged out of detention.

Fast-forward to Dr. Number One, a handsome, black-haired thirty-year-old in a white lab coat, which I know Mother Mary secretly covets.

All the doctors have their names embroidered on their lab coats, and her lab coat doesn't say anything except Dollar Store.

We all hold our breath as the young doctor sits down in front of Mother Mary to ask her a few questions. He begins, "First question. Where are you?"

Mother Mary snorts. "Where do you think I am?"

Watching, I say nothing. None of us is allowed to say anything. Nor are we allowed to coach or bribe her into submission, so we sit mute and still.

Dr. Number One tries again. "Second question. Who is the President of the United States?"

"What's the difference?"

I try not to watch. My mother is flunking cooperativeness, but the handsome doctor is smiling.

"Third question. Do you understand why you—"

"Wait." Mother Mary interrupts, holding up a gnarled finger. "I like you. You're cute. Did you meet my granddaughter?"

So you see where this is going. Mother Mary actually passes the first evaluation, though Francesca is not engaged to the young doctor. In fact, we all thought he was gay and tried to hook him up with Brother Frank, but we struck out with equality.

Later that day, Dr. Number Two enters the room, to administer Mother Mary's final test. Unlike the first doctor, he doesn't have the warmest bedside manner. On the contrary, he strides into the office, steely-haired and wire-rimmed. He sits down in front of Mother Mary, introduces himself, and is about to ask his first question when a neatly dressed woman appears in the doorway, from a room down the hall.

"Doctor," she says in an imperious way, "my husband has a question for you."

Dr. Number Two lifts an eyebrow. "I'll be back when I'm finished with this patient."

The woman vanishes with an unhappy frown, and Dr. Number Two returns his attention to Mother Mary. He's about to ask his first question, but she stops him.

"Where the hell does that broad get off?"

Doctor Number Two smiles.

And Mother Mary is in.

# Third Month's the Charm

By Francesca

I'm three months into a new relationship and living a charmed existence. Wherever we go, whatever we do, things just seem to work out for us. A free cab is turning around the corner, our discount tickets happen to be center orchestra, and the best table in the restaurant is just paying their bill.

We have such good luck, I feel guilty, which proves I'm my mother's daughter.

"So how was last night?" my mom said into the phone one morning. I hadn't told her I'd had a date, but she infers it whenever I miss her regular good-night phone call.

She is a mystery writer, after all.

At least she stopped presuming me dead.

"It was perfect, we had the best night."

I recounted how we walked the High Line, a beautiful park built over an old elevated railroad track that runs along the west side of lower Manhattan. It features gorgeous wildflowers, modern-art installations, and yummy food stands. My boyfriend got held up and had to push back our meeting time, but in doing so, we found ourselves walking the urban boardwalk just as the tangerine sun was setting over the shimmering waters of the Hudson.

" 'Tangerine sun?' " my mom said. "Geez, you are in love."

"Oh fine, it was orange. Anyway . . ."

We walked to the very end of the High Line and descended in an area of the city neither of us knew very well. On a whim, I mentioned being in the mood for sushi, and as if by magic, we spotted a tiny, authentic Japanese pub.

"Ooh, what did you have?" my mom asked.

She always asks me this. First, she likes to know I'm well fed, and second, she wants to vicariously eat it. Some mothers try to live through their daughters' youth or romance; I'm lucky my mom covets only my menus.

"We had salty edamame, fresh yellowtail sushi—"

"Yes . . ."

"And chewy soba noodles—"

"*Yes* . . ."

"And grilled whole squid."

"Ew."

"No, it was amazing."

"Well, it sounds very New York-y. I'm happy things are going so well. How did you get home, did you take a cab?"

She hates for me to take the subway at night. She even hates it in the past tense; that I survived to tell the tale is no comfort.

This time she didn't have to worry, even retroactively.

It was such nice weather, we decided to walk. We were hand in hand, retelling the story of how we met to one another, as if we weren't both there.

"Barf, right?" I interrupted myself.

"No, that's cute. Go on."

And we got the idea to take the High Line back. Technically, it closes at 10 P.M., and it was 10:04, but we figured they'd need time to clear it off—just enough time for us to sneak on. So, feeling giddy with our minor trespass, we raced up the steps.

Once up on the darkened pathway, I noticed some unusual fauna.

"Look at this beetle," I said, pointing to a black insect. "There are a couple of them over here."

"That's not a beetle," my boyfriend said. "That's a roach."

Squinting in the darkness, we saw hundreds of them, dark spots darting all across the walkway. The High Line was overrun with roaches.

Maybe this is why they close at ten.

It was like something out of a horror movie, and we were totally the sucker couple doomed to die in the first five minutes.

"Why are there so many?" I asked, leaping to avoid crunching the things.

"Maybe they're tourist roaches," he said, gleefully mowing them down.

We scampered to the nearest stairway down, doing our best tourist-roach impressions in various foreign accents.

"That's revolting," my mom said into the phone.

"No, it was funny! He's a really good mimic."

The rest of the way, we stayed safe at sea level. We even found a cute park to cut through, which was lovely save for the giant rat that crossed our path.

I wasn't so grossed out by that, because initially I thought it was a small cat.

We strolled the rest of the way along the river, with the Lite-Brite skyline of New Jersey twinkling from across the Hudson.

"That's better," my mom said.

"We did see two people shooting up. That was sad."

"*What?*"

Actually, I didn't see them, my boyfriend pointed them out once we were past.

"He joked that he wanted to show me 'Old New York,' isn't that clever?"

My mom was unamused.

"That aside, it was a perfect night."

"Geez." She laughed.

See what I mean?

Charmed.

# The Scent of a Woman

By Lisa

My house smells like dogs, but I smell like gardenias.

And wisteria, grapefruit, and tea roses.

Also opium. At least that's what it says on the bottle, and I'll take his word for it, since he's Yves St. Laurent.

I'm an Opium addict.

Today we're talking about perfume, and I'll explain why.

We begin when I get together for a weekly trail ride with my pals Nan and Paula. We call it a trail ride, but it's more like a trail sit. Nan is an expert horsewoman, but Paula and I are too scared to go faster than we can talk.

Horseback riding is great exercise, when other people do it. When I do it, it's excellent conversation.

The three of us talk about our kids, our lives, and our diets, but somehow this time, the subject turns to perfume, and as it happens, I'm the only one who wears it every day. They're both surprised, and come to think of it, so am I.

Loyal readers will recall that I'm your favorite dirtbag.

To be specific, I have confessed in these pages that I shower only every few days, wear the same black sweatpants throughout the winter, and have been known to sleep in my clothes.

With dogs.

Impressed yet?

The only excuse is that I work at home. If I'm doing my job, I don't meet anyone all day, except two thousand new words.

So naturally I don't wear makeup very often and if I go out to food-shop or run errands, I don't bother with mascara or eyeliner.

I was never a girly-girl, and now I've aged out of the category.

But the one thing that I always do, even at home, is wear perfume.

Every day.

I'm not quirky, I'm fragrant.

I think it started way back, because Mother Mary always wore perfume. She also smoked, so most of the time she smelled of Youth Dew and More 100s. I used to borrow her clothes in middle school, and I smelled generally older and wiser, or like a pack-a-day habit.

But a habit was born, which was being aromatic.

So I tried to sell Nan and Paula on wearing perfume. It makes you feel pretty even if you look like hell. It makes you feel elegant in a T-shirt. It makes you feel young when you're, well, my age.

Our sense of smell is one of only five senses, but it gets the least love.

We worry about what we look like, but little about what we smell like, and we can't even see what we look like. Fragrance can be for others, but it can also be just for us.

Perfume is personal aromatherapy.

So the next time my girlfriends and I went for a trail ride, I brought along three bottles of my favorite perfumes, like a taste test for women. I brought one that smells like roses, one that smells like spices, and one that smells vaguely powerful. We mixed and matched and had a great time, spraying ourselves before we got on the horses, right in the barn.

The horses were not amused. They're used to us spritzing fly spray, not perfume, which, oddly, worked almost as well at repelling flies.

I'm hoping men don't feel the same way.

Anyway, the horses were repulsed. They kept looking back at us as we rode, and Buddy The Pony threw his head high and curled his upper lip. This is called pflamen, which is something horses do when they don't like a smell.

I didn't take it personally.

The only smell Buddy likes is Eau de Carrots.

Anyway, that day, we decided that there was one perfume we liked the best.

The powerful one.

It smells like self-esteem in a bottle.

And no, I don't want to say the name of the perfume.

Whatever makes you feel powerful is up to you.

# With Apologies to L'Oreal

By Lisa

I'm sweltering because I have low self-esteem.

That's what I figured out.

Otherwise I can't explain my own dumb behavior.

This might be a new low, because usually I can explain my dumb behavior. Like if someone says, do you want to get married, I always say, Yes!

Dumb, but I know why.

Temporary insanity.

This time, I don't, and the stakes are much higher. We're talking air-conditioning.

We begin when summer started, in earnest. The heat wave rolled in with temperatures of ninety degrees, but for some reason, I don't turn on the air-conditioning. One part of my house has central air, and it happens to be where the family room and my office are, but still I can't bring myself to turn it on. By habit, I try not to turn on the air-conditioning unless I absolutely have to.

Dumb.

I tough it out. It's warm but not unbearable. I drink lots of iced drinks and wear tank tops and shorts. I tell myself I feel cool, even though the dogs pant and flop listlessly on the floor, flat as area rugs.

The cats don't mince words. They walk around with signs that read: TURN ON THE AC, DUMMY.

I know if I had a window air conditioner, I'd feel differently. Then I would turn it on and it would cool down the one room I was in and nothing else. But central air has to cool the family room, kitchen, and office—all for one person.

Me.

When Daughter Francesca lived at home, I would turn it on all the time. It makes sense, for two people.

But for one?

Me?

I sweat as I type away, and I'm on deadline, running out of steam. Still I think if I could just hang in a little longer, I could get through another day. Partly it's the money, because the bill is so high, but it was high for two people, too, so that can't be the real reason. It's not the money, but it seems wasteful.

For me alone.

Do you remember the commercial for L'Oreal hair color, where the tagline said, Because you're worth it?

I'll explain, for those under seventy years old.

The idea was that L'Oreal was the most expensive of the at-home hair-color kits, costing, if I remember correctly, twelve bucks a box.

Yes, there was a time when things cost twelve dollars.

And yes, there was a time when I did my own hair color, and it looked it. I was a Nice 'N Easy fan, which went for six bucks and was neither nice nor easy.

They also called it hair painting, and we all know what a lousy painter I am. I'm the girl who paints around the pictures on the wall, so you can imagine what my roots looked like.

**Boone bows to the fan in the absence of air-conditioning.**

Picasso.

By the way, L'Oreal doesn't use that tagline anymore, though its website asks, What Does Your Hair Color Say About You?

Which, I realized, is a more tactful way of saying, WHY DON'T YOU TURN ON THE AC, DUMMY?

I didn't spring for the L'Oreal, and frankly, I don't turn on the air-conditioning because, at some, level, I don't feel worth it.

Really?

Me?

Advocate of strong, independent women everywhere? Writer of books featuring same? Could I really have self-esteem that low?

Ouch.

I don't know the answer, and I don't want to know, but I turned on the air-conditioning immediately, just to prove it to myself that I wasn't a loser.

The dogs thanked me.

The cats didn't.

They knew they were worth it, all along.

# Bon Voyage?

---

By Francesca

Tomorrow I leave for vacation with my boyfriend. I was crazy excited about it, until I started packing.

Then I just went crazy.

My suitcase turned into a Pandora's box of worries, stress, and expectations.

We've never been on a trip together. Actually, I've never been on a trip with any boyfriend ever. But thanks to women's magazines, seventeen seasons of *The Bachelor,* and other people's Facebook feeds, I'm an expert on how to do it right. Every girl is. We are acutely aware of how we should look, act, and feel in almost every situation.

And if we know how we *should* be, then anything else is just lazy.

So even though this is my first trip with a boyfriend, I became determined to be awesome at it.

I want to be the *Dolce Vita* version of myself. I should be the type of woman who wears a dress and espadrilles to go biking, who sports a silk head scarf and earrings on the beach.

This was my Great Romantic Getaway, and I should look the part.

My boyfriend certainly didn't put this pressure on me; he

doesn't sweat this stuff. He will be traveling in Europe for work for over a month and he's only bringing a carry-on. I am joining him for two weeks, and I might need a carry-on for my shoes.

But that's to be expected. My boyfriend's wardrobe could be described as spartan chic—not that it is filled with leather and loincloths (I wish), but that it contains a sensible option for most occasions and not a thing more. The five dress shirts hung up in his closet have so much room to breathe—they look like they're for sale.

Meanwhile, my closet is vomiting hangers. My excuse is that my apartment closet is tiny, but it might also be because I throw nothing away.

Who knows? Someday I may want that pink dress I wore to the eighth-grade dinner dance.

When I can't find space on the rack to hang something, I wedge the new hanger in between the others and it stays in place.

Joan Crawford's head would explode.

Finding things, much less paring it down for a suitcase, was no easy task.

First, I auditioned each of my bathing suits to see which I felt the most confident in and I didn't feel confident in any.

So I packed them all.

I can diet on the plane.

Then I started trying on jeans to find the pair that were washed recently enough to be cute, but not so recently as to be sausage casing.

I set to work hand-washing the good bras while trying in vain to hunt down the long lost matching bottoms.

*Oh right,* I remembered. *I'm too cheap to buy matching bottoms in the first place.*

I wondered how late Victoria's Secret was open.

In my Boy-Scout frenzy of preparedness, I envisioned every possible occasion short of a red carpet and packed accordingly. Before I knew it, my closet was clean.

The Leaning Tower of Pisa erupting from my suitcase was another story.

This was so unlike me. I'm usually low-maintenance. My bathroom mirror is the only one in my entire apartment, and I only use the blow dryer on the dog after his bath.

But I had lost all sense of perspective; everything had to be perfect—I had to be perfect. On my new mental checklist of insecurity, it seemed of critical importance that I find a sunscreen that won't make my face look like an oil slick.

I rushed to the mall for emergency cosmetics. The saleswoman showed me a foundation with sunscreen that called itself "Camera Ready."

Something about the name gave me pause.

Is that what I really want to be?

Camera ready?

"It will hold up all day," the saleswoman said. "It was developed by makeup artists for *models*."

When models go somewhere exotic, it isn't vacation. It's work.

This trip is supposed to be my reward from working, but I had turned it into a job.

Sure, I want to look good, but mostly I want to explore and taste and see and do.

I want verbs, not adjectives.

I'd like to create great memories, not perfect pictures.

This trip isn't an audition, or a job, or a test.

It's a treat.

It should be fun.

Now that's a "should" I can get behind.

# In Which I Officially Hit the Wall!

By Lisa

I used to have a good attitude about getting older. I felt smarter and better than ever before, and I believed that my rich and varied life experience offset whatever age and gravity have done to my looks.

Well, forget it.

Because that was when I was fifty-six.

I'm about to turn fifty-seven.

And you know what's happening?

I'm hitting the wall.

I didn't even see it coming. I drove right into it, even though I was paying attention. I wasn't drunk or texting, and I even had my high beams on.

Though my high beams are lower than they used to be.

I'm thinking that this is how it must happen. Aging hits you like a head-on collision. Because all of a sudden, there it was, smack in my face.

There was no air bag, only an old bag.

Me.

Let's be real.

We use the term "hitting the wall" in this context, but it's not easy to find out exactly what it means. I looked through the conventional dictionaries for a definition of "hitting the wall," and they defined it as an idiom for "exercising to the point of exhaustion" or "running out of glycogen."

You have to be an idiot to believe that idiom.

And neither applies to me.

I'm at the point of exhaustion before I even start exercising, and I never have any glycogen, unless it comes in gummi.

Then I found another dictionary that defined "hitting the wall" as the point at which "one cannot make any further progress," which is close but no cigars.

I'm making enough progress.

But I'm looking like Methuselah.

Also, one sports dictionary said that a synonym for "hitting the wall," in bicycling, is "bonking."

But that's not what I'm talking about.

Though I'm betting that if you've hit the wall, you're not getting bonked.

Uh, bingo.

Then I dug a little deeper and found a website called urban-dictionary.com, which bills itself as "the dictionary that YOU wrote!"

Yay!

We've officially reached an all-time low in our culture, if a word's definition can be whatever any anonymous person says it is. This would be like having your facts checked by *Family Feud*.

Because, to give credit where it's due, the urban dictionary defined "hitting the wall," thusly:

"The point at which a girl that used to be hot is no longer hot. This is typically due to advancing age."

BAM!

Feel that?

It was the wall.

Not politically correct, but true.

And here is the example they gave, verbatim: "Heather Locklear has finally hit the wall. She must be over 40 now."

I'm not making this up.

Don't tell Heather Locklear.

She won't be able to hear you anyway, as she is over forty and will have to turn up her hearing aid.

By the way, please note that, according to urbandictionary .com, men don't hit the wall.

Women, start posting now.

Other terms we use to talk about aging are equally ouchy. For example, we say that we "look good for our age."

Okay, that might not be the best turn of phrase. It implies that if we looked our age, we would look bad. Like our age is a big secret, which it isn't, at least not for me. I'm pretty sure that my wrinkles spell fifty-seven.

And it ain't pretty.

Plus it's a losing battle. Gloria Steinem famously said, this is what fifty looks like, but she looked good for her age.

And she hadn't hit the wall.

The urban dictionary gives helpful synonyms for "hit the wall," which include "busted," "tore up," "haggard," "lost it," and "used up."

Yikes.

Still, you know the ones that are missing?

Alive!

Happy!

Healthy!

Lucky!

I may have hit the wall, but it didn't stop me. Which defies the definitions of the urban dictionary as well as the laws of physics.

Happy Birthday, to all of us who are alive, happy, and healthy.

We're lucky.

Whether we're hot or not.

# William Wordsworth Needs a New Password

By Lisa

I pay my bills the old-fashioned way, which is to say I put a check in an envelope, use a stamp, and stick it in a mailbox, to be lost by the postal service.

All my adult life, my habit has been to sit down once a month, during the last week of the month, and pay my bills. I'm lucky enough these days to be able to pay them all, which was not always the case, when mortgage and utilities got first dibs. I used the Monopoly System of Home Finance, which was that only monopolies got paid.

I even pay down my credit cards completely, to avoid interest charges. You may recall that I charge everything possible, so I can collect reward points with which I can buy vacuum cleaners I won't use and spices I don't like.

But they're free, so you can't beat the price.

Still, even though I have the money, I hate the day I pay my bills. It's like tax day, every month. Who likes to pay the piper? Nobody, and he charges too much.

Until recently, my bill-paying system was working fine, but lately my VISA card has been getting declined left and right, which is always a nice moment, especially in a crowded grocery store. You really don't want to be the person saying, "I'm sure I paid that."

Nobody believes you.

They're all thinking, "No way she paid that."

And then you get to say, "I have another card."

But everyone is thinking, "That one won't work either. She might be a crack addict. Look at her hair. Also I think she slept in those sweatpants."

So this happens enough times that I have a few cranky calls with my VISA card company, which seems not to have made my acquaintance, though I've sent them a small fortune each month for the last fifteen years. They say they keep declining the card because my payments were respectively one, one, and two days late for the past three months. The fact that we've been together forever doesn't matter.

I've divorced men for less.

And the VISA card company isn't the only bad husband.

I keep getting notices that threaten to turn off my electricity, and I don't understand that either, because I paid that bill, too. So I looked again at the last bill and realized that I got it about thirty seconds before it was due. I was late to pay it before I even received it, which might be a land-speed record for financial shenanigans.

Finally, when I was about to get my bunion surgery a few months ago, I actually learned that my health insurance was in default because it hadn't been paid in two months. But I knew I paid that. And it turned out that for a reason the insurance company can't explain, my bills get sent to me every two months, not every month, and if I happen to miss paying a bill, which does happen from time to time, I am already two months behind. Don't ask me why they don't send it monthly, but it's one of the reasons I hate my health-insurance company.

And so does everybody else.

I tell my friends these troubles, and they say I have to pay my bills more often, as soon as they come in, and that online bill pay will make this easier. So I go to my bank's site, and it tells me it needs my social security number, my account number, and my VISA Check Card Number. But I don't have a VISA Check Card, and the fine print says if you didn't have such a card, to call a certain phone number, which I did. Then the mechanical operator asked me for my user name, which I didn't know, and my telephone bill-paying PIN, which I didn't have.

So I hung up.

I'm going to print out a bunch of checks right now, so they'll be ready when the bills get here. I will stand at the mailbox like a dog and pay each bill the moment it arrives. I will pay for lights I haven't turned on yet and shoes I haven't even seen in stores.

I will turn every day of my life into tax day.

William Wordsworth said the world is too much with us, and he was right.

He didn't have online bill pay, either.

# Love and Marriage, Then Divorce

―――――――――

By Lisa

It should be clear by now that I know nothing about love or marriage.

But about divorce, I'm an expert.

Or so I thought.

Ask me anything, I used to think. I could've written a book. In fact, I always thought I would or I had, like twenty, but never mind, I've come to understand I don't know anything about love, marriage, or even divorce.

The reasons?

Tom and Katie.

I'm a Tom Cruise fan, and so is Daughter Francesca. As you may remember from our previous book, we have Tom Cruise Appreciation Week, especially during power outages, when we watch his movies on laptops. And I remember very well when Tom fell in love with Katie Holmes and jumped on Oprah's couch.

You know what I thought?

Yay!

Good for him!

He's happy and in love!

Yes, I am the only person in America who did NOT think

it was weird that he got so excited he jumped on the couch. Number one, I'm Italian, and we get excited easily. If somebody brings us a plate of spaghetti, it's all we can do not to jump on the couch.

We like it. Couches, spaghetti, everything. We're excitable.

But even so, I still don't think it's crazy he jumped on the couch for love. I myself, your favorite celibate, have felt like jumping on couches for love.

Why not?

Couches have cushions for a reason.

And the guy was happy.

An entire nation called him weird, but secretly, I was jealous. I hoped that someday, somebody would jump on a couch for me and be called weird by an entire nation.

So I admit, I was out of the mainstream on that one, which happens sometimes, and we all live. But the very next time I was completely out of the mainstream was when Tom and Katie announced they were separating, and nobody was surprised.

Except me.

I was *astounded*.

I heard it on TV and I thought something was wrong with the set. I couldn't believe it. They were so cute together and the kid is adorable, and so are the other kids, and they seemed like such a happy family.

Suffice it to say, I didn't see it coming. I don't know why they got divorced, and that isn't my point herein. Rumor has it the reason is Scientology, but I don't know anything about Scientology except that it's kind of a dumb word. I have no view of Scientology and I don't poke fun at other people's religions, because believers will kill me in its name.

I was still working through the fact of Tom and Katie's separation when they announced they were divorced.

WHAT?

Now I'm really confused.

Because I grant that I know nothing about love or marriage, but about divorce I know everything, especially that it takes FOREVER and costs A BILLION DOLLARS.

Tom and Katie went through separation to divorce in eleven days.

That's not possible. They divided a couple of kids, massive amounts of money, several houses, plenty of cars, and more than one couch.

In eleven days!

In eleven days, I can't pick a paint color.

If you ask me, this is a disaster. It contravenes all we know and hold dear about divorce, namely that it's absurdly expensive and insanely painful. If people can go from married to divorced in eleven days, the problem is obvious.

It's going to put a lot of divorce lawyers out of business.

They're going to be out roaming the streets, with time on their hands.

Can you imagine lawyers walking around, with nothing to do?

It can only end badly, my friends.

So now I fear for our nation.

But not Tom.

He will be okay.

In fact, he will come and save the world.

I know, I saw it in the movies.

# You Say Tomato

---

By Lisa

Did you hear about this?

I read in the newspaper that somebody noticed that red tomatoes sell better than greenish ones, so food engineers started changing the genetic makeup of tomatoes to make them redder, except that it also took out the taste.

I learned so much from this that I don't know where to begin.

Number one, food has engineers?

I thought trains had engineers, and food had cooks.

I just went from choo-choo to chew-chew.

In fact, I thought you had to have an engine to have an engineer, but no.

If you ask me, this opens new job opportunities for engineers. For example, I see a lot of trees that could use a good engineer. They aren't green enough, especially in fall, when they turn a lot of crazy colors that don't match.

I mean, let's be real. Yellow and red? Nobody looks good in yellow and red, except Ronald MacDonald.

He's single for a reason.

Worse, in winter, the leaves on the trees actually fall off. That's definitely an engineering problem. I feel pretty sure a tree engineer would fix that, no sweat.

Also the sun.

Don't get me started on the sun. It's supposed to be yellow, but it's too bright to tell the color. In fact, it's so bright that we have to buy dark glasses to even be around it.

Also the sun is hot, which can be a bummer. It makes us feel listless and uncomfortable, then we have to turn on the air-conditioning, or at least decide whether or not to, which can be a problematic choice for certain people, involving money and self-esteem, oddly intertwined.

Not that I know anyone like that.

And also in winter, the sky could use a good engineer. There are times when it changes from blue to a very boring whitish gray, then actually breaks up and falls to the ground in tiny, cold pieces that we all have to clean up.

Needs work.

Sky engineers should get on it. It's like the sky doesn't even stay up, which is a major engineering defect. Cantilevers, buttressing, and scaffolding may be required, and lots of it.

Really, lots.

Or worse, sometimes the sky loses its blue color, turns gray, but doesn't break up and fall to the ground, right after I spent hundreds of dollars on a green machine to help me clean up the pieces.

That's a lot of green, even for a green machine.

Who knew that colors required so much engineering? If you ask me, green is the color most in need of engineering. I wish those engineers who were trying to fix the tomatoes would fix the economy, but never mind, what do I know?

Let's move on to my second point.

Having been astounded to learn that tomatoes have engineers, I was also amazed to learn that they had genes, too.

Who knew tomatoes were so busy?

I grow tomatoes, and I haven't given them the credit they deserve for their rich inner lives.

To be honest, I had no idea that food had genes, at all. Just like I thought you needed an engine to have an engineer, I thought you needed, like, blood and a heart to have genes.

It's hard enough for me to remember that a tomato is a fruit, not a vegetable, but now I'm expected to know it has DNA, as well?

Bottom line, I'm bad at biology. Anyone who's slept with me will tell you that.

But now we know that tomatoes have genes, this opens up new job opportunities, namely for actors. Think of all the new TV shows this could create, like *CSI: Tomatoes,* where they collect tomato DNA to catch the killer tomato.

In fact, we could have murders for every fruit, then spin it off to vegetables, too.

*To Catch a Salad Shooter.*

# Call of Jury Duty

---

By Francesca

When I received the summons for jury duty, I didn't know what to expect. Turns out, jury duty is a lot like high school.

While our instructor was taking attendance, I felt like I was back in homeroom. Everyone was sleepy, grumpy, and seated in a collective slump. There were posters on the wall picturing a perfectly diverse group of smiling people, only instead of "Knowledge is Power," it had fine print about doing your civic duty.

I don't know how much motivation you need to do something that's compulsory.

The instructor told us to correct him if he was mispronouncing any names then proceeded to mispronounce all of them. There was that one person who waited three beats before saying "Here," and the person who made a point to say, "Present," instead. Each time he came upon a no-show, I had to fight the urge to say "Bueller, Bueller?"

When a short lunch break was announced, there was a stampede out of the courthouse. Eating on campus was clearly uncool.

After a quick hunt for cheap fare, I ducked into a sandwich shop. The place had only a few café tables, all taken. A man sitting alone said I was welcome to join him, and after hesitating, I did a very un–New Yorker thing—I accepted.

"Thanks, I'm on break from jury duty."

"Me too," he said. And suddenly we were pals, griping about the lawyers, comparing cases, talking about our dogs.

I hadn't been this happy to have someone to sit with at lunch since sixth grade.

Before we knew it, recess was over. Back at the courthouse, we were divided into smaller jury pools and sent to be questioned by the lawyers for each side in a process known as *voir dire*. French class all over again.

The defense lawyer was an older Asian man with the voice and demeanor of Joe Pesci. If you had any issues with authority, he was the type of guy you'd want to punch. On the other hand, the plaintiff's attorney was a young woman, earnest but apologetic. She was the student teacher about to get torn to shreds.

Every time the lawyers stepped outside to argue, which was often, we erupted in chatter, gossip, and imitations of them, making the most of our unsupervised minutes. But as soon as the door would open, we'd snap back into the little angels that we weren't.

And although our group was as varied as Manhattan itself, with every age, race, and profession imaginable, when it came to types, the room could've been cast by John Hughes.

We had the long-haired guy who sat in the back, brooding and mysterious. When I was sixteen, I dated that guy. This time, he didn't even make me a mix CD.

There was the popular girl, with long, shiny blond hair, who already seemed to have made friends. She was like Marcia Brady with a better sense of humor and an advanced degree. I wanted to braid her hair.

The hot-girl foreign-exchange student. When a young,

very pretty Hispanic woman asked the lawyer to define "hoarder," every Spanish-speaking male jumped to help her.

Our class clown was sitting next to me in the back. He was smart, funny, and a little mischievous.

He just happened to be seventy-eight years old.

Once, when one of the lawyers asked a particularly vague, roundabout question, he called out, "Do you believe in Manifest Destiny?"

Everyone laughed, but the attorney didn't appreciate his class participation.

The one difference from high school was the sense of camaraderie. A jury, by its very nature, makes peers of people who may seem completely different. Initially, I thought it was because we were all stuck in this chore together. But despite our

Because of his priors, Pip is not eligible for jury duty.

shenanigans when the teacher's back was turned, during the questioning, people took it seriously, answered honestly, and rose to the occasion. Because we'd want someone to do the same for us.

Ultimately, I was not chosen for the trial. But at the end of the day, I rode the subway home with my new friend, a seventy-eight-year-old smart-aleck, and I felt lucky we were stuck in this city, and this nation, together.

# To Catch a Predator

---

By Lisa

I have a crush.

On a fox.

Literally.

What can I say?

He's foxy.

Let me explain.

A few months ago, I noticed that there was a baby fox running around my backyard, hanging out in some brush to the left, far from the house. He was red, fluffy, and adorable, with delicate black paws and ears, and I began to spend time watching him.

That makes me sound lonelier than I am.

Also creepier, especially when I use my binoculars.

If I get a GPS on him, call the authorities.

In time, the fox grew up, going from cute to handsome and then some. Imagine Justin Bieber turning into Hugh Jackman, like Wolverine, only nice.

A stone fox.

His body got fuller, his coat glossier, and he sprouted a thick patch of white fur on his chest.

I like chest hair, even if it's white.

I'm at that age.

In my own defense, I also like nature, especially when it can be even remotely classified as a Woodland Creature.

Chipmunks, call me.

Also I loved that animated movie *The Fantastic Mr. Fox,* so it was all I could do not to catch the fox and dress him in a pin-striped suit. In case you were wondering, my thing for the fox has nothing to do with the fact that George Clooney voiced the fox in *The Fantastic Mr. Fox.* As we know, I'm over my crush on George and have moved on to Bradley Cooper, because crushes are highly transferrable, especially when they're completely imaginary.

And also this is one smart fox.

I didn't know that foxes really were smart, but believe the hype.

He darts away if I go out the back door, then sticks his head up from the brush when I go inside, as if he watches my comings and goings. He comes out only at certain times of the evening, when we sit and stare at each other from across the lawn. I begin to notice that I'm looking forward to our end-of-the-day staring sessions.

In other words, dates.

Words aren't always necessary between us.

Frankly, I've had entire marriages that were far less interesting.

By the way, foxes mate for life.

Unlike me.

My fox is so cool and elusive, the ultimate mystery man. Either he has intimacy issues, or I do.

Daughter Francesca came home to visit, and I showed her the fox, but she frowned. "Mom," she said, "he's cute, but stay away."

"I know, he could have herpes."

"You mean rabies."

"Right." I meant rabies. "I was wondering if I should put some food out for him."

Francesca's eyes widened. "Are you serious? He's a predator."

"So what? They have to eat, too."

"You *want* him around?"

"Of course. Isn't he great? I mean, he's like another dog and cat, combined." I didn't tell her he's my crush. I didn't want her to think I like bad boys.

So I didn't feed him, because my daughter is smarter than I am.

But neither of us is as smart as my fox.

I say this because the other day he ran by with a bird in his mouth, and I realized that it might have come from my bird feeder by the back door, which I keep full because I like to watch birds, too.

Though with them I manage to check my romantic urges.

No chest hair.

Although yesterday I did see a superhot blue jay.

Anyway I felt terrible about the bird who was about to be dinner, and worse about the fox. And now I'm thinking that all this time, on our nightly dates, the fox wasn't watching me, but the bird feeder.

He wasn't the man I thought he was.

# Dog Years

---

By Lisa

It's time to acknowledge that, a few weeks ago, we lost our golden retriever, Penny.

You don't have to acknowledge it, but I do. Nothing for me is real until I write about it, so now it's official.

And heartbreaking.

She was thirteen and playing fetch until the day she passed, of natural causes, at home in my arms. She died resting in the very spot in the entrance hall where she guarded the house.

No golden is much of a guard dog, and Penny was the worst guard dog ever. And the best dog ever.

She loved everything and everybody, and she was small for a golden, with bright, dark eyes and a tongue as pink as a petal.

If petals slobbered.

She passed lying in the sun, which was as she lived.

Always in the sun, this one.

She was special, but all dogs are special in their own way.

She was the daughter of Lucy, our big red golden retriever, and the half sister of Angie, our middle golden retriever.

Yes, I'm one of those people who talks about their dogs like family.

Because they are.

But my point is that we got Lucy when Daughter Francesca was eight years old, and when Francesca was thirteen, Lucy gave birth to Penny. We acquired Angie somewhere in between, so bottom line, we had golden retrievers for almost nineteen years.

The golden years.

The three of them frolicked around the house, snored nosily, chased Kong balls, swam like crazy, and jumped in the car for rides when they weren't begging for cake, bread, or leftover spaghetti.

Scottolines love carbohydrates.

They made a matched set of small, medium, and large, which was respectively Penny, Angie, and Lucy, on account of all that spaghetti. They roamed the house and yard like a furry trio, a doggie trifecta, or The Three Amigos.

We thought and spoke of them in one word, LucyAngie-Penny.

Until they began to pass, one by one.

Only death could separate them.

Though their remains are upstairs on shelves with those of our other pets, a row of small cedar chests that are displacing the books. Soon I'll have my own TV show on A&E, entitled *People Who Hoard Dog, Cat, and Horse Ashes.*

It's not a home office, it's a home mausoleum.

I even save the sympathy cards that my wonderful vet sends me with the chests, because I actually find comfort in that stuff about the Rainbow Bridge, which I believe is right off of I-95. And like a big dork, I posted Penny's photo on Facebook and Twitter, then cried my way through all the lovely comments.

It's the people who get us through the dogs.

In some ways, Penny was the hardest to lose, not only because she was the last, but also she was the baby of the family, born in this house, the smallest of Lucy's puppies, in a litter of nine.

Penny was the scrappy runt who grew into a charmer. Her full name was Lucky Penny.

And her passing is the end of an era.

Losing Penny taught me that we love a dog for her own sake, but we also associate them with the times of our lives, and so their loss brings into relief our own passage of time.

The golden years were Francesca's coming of age, and my forties and early fifties.

My coming of middle age.

Somewhere in between these wonderful dogs was a disas-

**Lucky Penny, the Golden Girl**

trous second divorce, so that my memory of that time is one of happy golden retrievers and an atomic bomb.

And now, happily and sadly, all that is past.

I don't mind getting older. Actually, I love it. What I mind is losing things I love.

I love and hate surviving.

Which is the ultimate lesson, after all.

Loss is part of life, and becomes more so as we grow older. Life contains the bitter and the sweet, and eventually itself becomes bittersweet.

Still, I'll take it.

I'm a lucky penny.

# I'm on It, Walt

by Lisa

Walt Whitman said, I sing the body electric.

So do I, Walt.

Because now I have an electronic face washer.

And it changed my life.

Looking back, my initiation into the electronic era started with an electronic toothbrush. It was recommended by my dental hygienist, as she was sandblasting my teeth.

"Buy one," she said, from behind her surgical mask. For me, she needs a surgical helmet. When my plaque starts flying, it's like shrapnel.

But at the time, the idea of an electronic toothbrush seemed crazy, because I used a toothbrush, powered by my flabby arms.

"Not good enough," she said. "Make sure you get the kind that says Elite."

So I bought the Elite toothbrush, took it home, and brushed my teeth. I used it for a month, driving it around my teeth, back and forth, up and down, producing lots of foamy suds. I saw some difference, and so did the dogs, who stopped complaining about my breath.

Dogs hate people breath.

So I was primed for the ads I began to see, for an electronic face washer. I snapped one up as soon as it became available, even though it wasn't cheap.

Why?

Because I can't be expected to wash my face all by myself.

That would be free, easy, and normal.

Also I read that the electronic face washer exfoliates your skin, and as all women know, exfoliates is the magic word.

We're talking pores, not napalm.

This is exfoliating, but in a good way, if you follow.

The face washer promised to polish off the dead skin on my face, and as such, it was calling my name, because my dead skin is really piling up. I might be a foot deep in dead skin. Like newfallen snow, you could stick a ruler in it and measure accumulation levels.

Come to think of it, maybe I could use that snowblower, after all.

I bought an electronic washer, which came in a set, one for the face and one for the body.

I gave the body one to Daughter Francesca, of course. I don't care about dead skin anywhere but where people can see it, and it goes without saying that nobody is seeing dead skin on my body.

Also I can't be bothered. I barely shave my legs anymore. I wait until spring.

For this reason, I will never move to California or Florida. I tell people I like the seasons, but what I really like is not bothering.

Anyway, I started using the electronic face washer, driving it around my face, back and forth, up and down, producing lots of foamy suds.

Foam = fun.

And miraculously, my skin began to look less dead. I told as much to Francesca, who loved it, too. But then she watched me wash my face, and smiled.

"Mom, you don't have to move it around that much when you use it."

"What?" I blinked.

"Did you read the directions?"

"Of course not. How long have you known me?" I never read the directions. I spent my whole life following directions, and now I can't be bothered. See? Told you.

"All you have to do is move it a little. It's sonic."

"No, it's not, it's electronic." I rinsed my face, confused.

"It's powered by electricity, but it cleans, sonically. It's made by Sonicare. It's sonic, like your toothbrush. You don't move that around, do you?"

"Sure. Up and down, over and out, lots of suds. Fun, fun, fun."

"You don't have to. Just hold it still and it does the work. Sonic."

I looked at the toothbrush and face washer, and realized that Francesca was right. It said Sonicare, but I had gotten distracted by the Elite.

Sorry, Walt.

I sing the body, supersonic.

# Stage Mom

---

By Francesca

I never thought I would be a stage mom, but as I envisioned my baby posing for a photographer, I couldn't help but feel a surge of vicarious excitement.

My dog was slated to star in an upcoming advertisement for the American Kennel Club's Meet the Breeds event at the Javits Center.

It started with an email from my dog's breeder and official Secretary of the Cavalier King Charles Spaniel Club of Delaware Valley, or CKCSCDV.

The acronym could use an abbreviation.

The breeder wrote me saying that the AKC's Meet the Breeds event was having a promotional photo shoot in a week's time and that the advertisement would feature only a Cavalier and a bulldog, "so I thought immediately of Pip, since he is so charismatic and photogenic."

My heart began to beat faster.

Then she wrote, "Pip's picture will be all over NYC and possibly the Northeast."

Now I was bouncing in my computer chair.

I was already seeing my dog's adorable face plastered on

flyers, brochures, posters, and—why not?—billboards up and down I-95.

This gig could be a stepping-stone for the cover of Milk-Bone boxes, maybe even a featured role on the next tear-jerking Purina dog chow ads.

Pip could be great! *So* so great!

I was slipping deep into a Mama Rose fantasy, when I remembered: I had just gotten Pip a short haircut. The classic Cavalier King Charles look has long fur or "feathers" on the ears, legs, and belly—none of which Pip currently possessed. The weather had been warm, so I'd gotten him groomed with his comfort in mind, not his show-dog potential.

What was I thinking?

I quickly wrote her back saying I'd love to do it, but I confessed to the minor hairstyle hiccup. She responded that she didn't think it'd be a problem, but asked for a picture of him to show the director.

I saw it as an audition.

Pip was curled up, sound asleep, on my couch, but I jostled him awake. I dragged an armchair across the room and positioned it in front of the window for the best natural light. Then I plopped Pip on the chair and encouraged him to look at me by holding one of his favorite liver treats.

I snapped the first pic on my iPhone.

He looked handsome, of course, but a little too intense. Perhaps the liver treat was a bad idea. I let him eat it before we tried again. This time I distracted him by waving my arm out to the side.

Soft eyes, Pip, soft eyes.

The second set was better, although half of his face was in shadow.

I considered the ethics of covertly running the photo through an Instagram filter before sending it to the breeder.

#overthinkingit.

I didn't end up altering any photos, but I did take about fifteen shots before settling on two to email back to her. One headshot, one full-body.

Thank God I'd had him on a diet all summer.

I emailed the photos and waited for her reply.

And waited.

I must have refreshed my Gmail account twenty times in two hours. Three days passed with no word, so I bit the bullet

**Rejected: Crazy Eyes**

and called her. She delivered the blow: The director decided to go with a "full-coated" dog.

I was crushed. I bit my lip and turned away from the phone. I didn't know how I'd break the news to Pip, who was asleep on the couch again.

"I understand," I said, trying not to sound as crestfallen as I was. "Well, you know, keep us in mind for next time."

But like any good stage mother, my disappointment curdled to indignation. How dare they overlook my baby's potential? One little haircut can't dull his sparkle. I can't walk this dog down the street without getting stopped by adoring passersby. You can't *groom* charisma, people. I don't need the stupid AKC's approval to know my dog is a star!

"I'll check back with you in February," said the breeder. "Maybe they can use him in the promotions for Westminster."

Westminster?

As in, the Westminster Kennel Club Dog Show, the oldest and most prestigious dog show in America?

Pip's lucky the weather's cooling down.

Because somebody's growing his hair out.

# Extra Extra Crispy

By Lisa

My faith in American ingenuity is restored.

We just invented fried butter.

Whew!

You may have been worried that we didn't have any more tricks up our sleeve, but you would be wrong. We used to invent things like electricity, heart valves, and polio vaccines, but we've finally come up with something useful.

Somebody at the Iowa State Fair developed a recipe for deep fried butter.

It sold like hotcakes.

Fried hotcakes.

What an idea! How else you gonna meet your daily cholesterol requirements?

They make it by freezing a stick of butter, dipping it in batter with cinnamon and sugar, deep-frying it in vegetable oil at 375 degrees, then drizzling it with a honey glaze.

You know you want one.

The other bestsellers at the state fair were deep-fried pickles, deep-fried corn dogs, and deep-fried macaroni and cheese.

I might move to Iowa.

Land where the tall corn (dogs) grow.

It's not just state fairs, either. My favorite fancy restaurant serves microgreens with fried goat cheese. Guess which I eat first, the microgreens or the fried cheese? Right, and thank God the fried cheese isn't micro.

Tell the truth. Who hasn't dived into a plate of fried mozzarella sticks?

Bottom line, it's time to concede that we love fried things. French fries, fried onion rings, fried chicken. And we don't just love fried food, we even love the fried part, all by itself.

Everybody on earth has nibbled the fry off of something.

Case in point, me.

Back in my non-vegetarian days, I used to love Kentucky Fried Chicken, extra crispy. Extra crispy was code for really really fried. When there was no more chicken left, I ate the nuggets of really really fried. Even after two days in the refrigerator, I ate delicious knots of crunchy, salty, really really fried.

The chicken was beside the point, because the only thing that mattered was the fried, and that's true with every fried food.

It tastes the same.

Fried.

Yay!

This is why I order shrimp tempura at a Japanese restaurant. Because all I taste is the fry, and I might as well be at Seafood Shanty.

Tempura is Japanese for corn dog.

We agree that frying will make a good thing better, but the truly amazing thing about frying is that it will make even disgusting things better.

Example?

Calamari.

It's a squid, for God's sake. Have you ever seen a squid? If you had, you wouldn't put it in your mouth.

But fry it, and people fight to get to it first.

Same thing with softshell crabs. A softshell is a crab that has recently molted its shell, so that its exoskeleton is still soft. You wouldn't normally eat a soft exoskeleton, much less all the stuff that's inside a crab, namely whatever he ate last.

Do you think crabs are picky eaters?

I don't.

So you have to factor that in.

Plus the eyes are still attached.

Enough said.

If you had to eat a softshell crab as is, you would refuse. Your better judgment would prevail.

But fried?

Everybody's there.

The proof is that people in Thailand eat fried bugs.

Now you know why.

Tastes like (fried) chicken.

The next step is only logical. If frying makes disgusting food delicious, there's no reason to stop at food, at all.

I'm not only thinking out of the box, I'm thinking out of the refrigerator.

If you can fry squid, you can fry flip-flops.

If you can fry butter, you can fry bark.

If you can fry bugs, you can fry Crestor.

And you're gonna have to.

# Ovarian Contrarian

By Lisa

They say this is the Year of the Woman.

Of course they're right.

Ever since we got the vote, we've been hell-bent for leather.

By the way, we got the vote ninety-two years ago.

Or Years-of-the-Woman ago.

To prove that The Year of the Woman is here, they point out that Augusta National Golf Club just allowed two women to join its membership, after eighty years of admitting only men. One woman, who led a protest at the club in 2003, said last week, "My first reaction was, we won—and we did."

That would be the reaction of a patient woman.

I'm not that patient.

To me, if you protested something in 2003 and they didn't do anything about it until 2012, you did not win.

Or to be precise, you did, but we could all be dead by then.

And if you had to wait eighty years to play golf, you might find a new sport.

By the way, Dr. Condoleezza Rice was one of the women admitted to Augusta. She became Secretary of State in 2005. So it was easier to join the Cabinet than a golf club.

This must be some club.

I'd like to club them.

More proof this is The Year of the Woman is that the National Football League just named its first female referee. She had been officiating for seventeen years, but fortunately, it's the Year of the Woman, so she got the job. She said, "Every step is hope that I can continue to show it really doesn't matter, male or female, as long as you work hard."

Which shows that she is patient.

Not me.

I would say that it really does matter, male or female. Because if you're male, you could have been a referee in the NFL since 1920, which is when the NFL started. But if you're female, you had to wait ninety-two years, for The Year of the Woman.

Rather, the Year of the Extremely Patient Woman.

They say the best proof that this is the Year of the Woman is the recent Olympics, where women won more gold medals than men. One newspaper headline read that "Title IX Made Women Gold Medalists Possible At 2012 Olympics." Interesting, because Title IX, which barred gender discrimination in education and sports, was enacted in 1972. The newspaper said, "it does not take Einstein to prove that Title IX has had a positive effect on women's athletics."

True.

But Einstein might also point out that Title IX was enacted forty years ago. And the Olympics were last week.

In fact, Einstein said time is relative, and he was right. Because, relatively speaking, forty years between the passing of a law and this result is way too long.

Bottom line, I'm coming to the conclusion that women are too patient, especially when it comes to themselves and their own needs and wishes.

We think justice delayed is justice denied, but only for others.

For example, our children. If our kid needs posterboard for

a school project that's due on Monday, guaranteed we're driving to Staples before it closes on Sunday night. And if they shut that door in our face, we'll get all Terms-of-Endearment on their heinie.

At times like that, we're not endearing.

So what?

But when it comes to us, we're enduring.

We're saints.

And I can't be the only woman who isn't ready to be beatified.

Who believes that sometimes, impatience is a virtue.

Who wants what I want when I want it.

Now.

It took me forever to learn the lesson that you can't wait forever.

I'm finally learning to ask as much for myself, and as quickly, as I do for Daughter Francesca or Mother Mary.

And to expect it.

So excuse me if I don't jump up and down because somebody is finally giving me what I deserved decades ago.

Time to change the model.

Because if nothing changes, nothing changes.

Let's make this The Year of the Impatient Woman.

Pronto.

# Saving Grace

---

By Lisa

I'm concerned that hoarding is getting a bad name.

And I blame cable.

I say this because I'm not a fan of clutter, but there are definitely things I save, even though I could end up on A&E.

Once again, it's not my fault.

Even my faults are not my fault.

Yes, that's the kind of grade-A attitude that got me divorced twice.

Don't try it at home.

In our culture, we get a mixed message about saving. It used to be that saving was a good thing. You saved time, you saved money, and you saved yourself for marriage.

Okay, I didn't save myself for marriage.

I didn't even save my marriage.

And both were excellent decisions.

Also in the olden days, someone who loved you wrote you love letters, and you saved them. When you stopped loving him and realized he was a jerk, you threw the letters away. Or burned them. Or showed them to your girlfriends and had a good laugh.

Not that I ever did this.

But it was fun.

To review, it used to be that saving was a good thing, and people were told to do more of it. When TVs broke, we repaired them, and when shoes wore out, we resoled them.

We saved our soles.

But no more.

When TVs break, we throw them away, and you'd travel far to find a shoe repair. Everything's disposable, and saving has become a bad thing, so I'm starting to look funny at the things I save, namely plastic bags, hotel soaps, and keys.

I can't be alone in this.

I don't know why I save plastic bags, but they do come in handy, and I end up with a ton at the end of the week. I rank them on a one-to-three scale, as in Yes, No, or Maybe So. I save the Yeses and the Maybe Sos.

See, I'm already starting to sound cable-ready.

But bear with me.

The bags from grocery stores are too thin, so they're a No, but the CVS bags are thicker and a pretty white, so they rank a Maybe So. The only solid Yes is the plastic bag from the Apple store, because they have actual drawstrings or better yet, can morph into a backpack.

How could you not save that? Don't you think it will come in handy, when you wear your plastic outfit?

I would bet money that nine out of ten women would save an Apple plastic bag if Bravo weren't watching.

And now, in California, they're telling you to save plastic bags and reuse them.

Recycling is politically correct hoarding.

Consider hotel soaps, which I love for their fragrance as well as their cuteness, shaped like miniature shells, balls, or bars, usually in pastel shades that scream guest bathroom. I save them though I'd never put them in the guest bathroom.

It's not impressive when your soaps say Hilton.

Especially if your towels say Ritz-Carlton.

Just kidding.

My only excuse for saving hotel soap is that I use it upstairs and don't have to buy bar soap as often. Never mind that few things are cheaper than bar soap. If you built a house of bar soap, it would cost you $36.75.

With a coupon.

The last thing I save is keys.

Truly, I don't know why. I have old keys everywhere in my house, from all the stages of my life, and I have no idea what they unlock, yet I cannot bring myself to throw them away.

I could get locked out.

Or locked in.

Which is worse, and who knows?

I should throw them away, and set myself free.

I smell a metaphor.

Or maybe that's the hotel soap.

# Be Careful What You Wish List

---

By Francesca

I just added a pair of Chloe flats to my Net-A-Porter.com "Wish List."

By the way, the shoes cost $495, which is $495 more than I have to spend on shoes. But that's okay, because I don't have any intention of buying them.

Isn't that how everyone uses online-shopping wish lists?

For those of you who prefer a life grounded in reality and don't know what I'm talking about, most online retailers allow users to save a list of desired items on a "wish list," a sort of shopping-cart purgatory.

I love using wish lists, because then the site notifies me if the price of one of my chosen items gets discounted from totally-ridiculously-expensive to get-real-you-still-can't-afford-it.

Okay, so maybe I'm doing it wrong.

But I don't really know how one is *supposed* to use a wish list. Most sites provide the option of emailing the wish list to some-one, but to whom? A mysterious benefactor? A sugar daddy? A blackmail victim?

But alas, I have moral integrity. So my wish list is for my eyes only. It doesn't matter that I'm no closer to owning that swishy Prada circle skirt, it feels like I am.

Call it aspirational online shopping.

It's the fantasy that I would buy clothes like these, just not now. I've even gone so far as to contact the live-chat customer service with a question about sizing for a bikini I could never afford.

You have to commit to the bit.

Eventually, the item on my wish list sells out or is no longer offered, and then I'm off the hook. Gosh, darn, better luck next time. My clicker finger gets some exercise, but my wallet doesn't starve.

I've invented passive willpower. Fiscal responsibility by forfeit.

Plus, I like getting credit for my excellent taste that goes into curating my wish list. Credit from whom, you ask?

The NSA must have some women working for them.

Mostly, I get credit from my best friend. We recently discovered that we both practice delusional wish-listing, so the last time she was over, we sat down and compared our lists, *ooh*ing and *ahh*ing over our collections of the very best pieces from each designer line.

It's like fantasy football, but with fashion.

My friend and I fantasy-shop for each other. I'll email her items I know she would love, despite a stratospheric price tag, with subject lines like: "Getting this for your birthday 2025."

By then, it might be on sale.

When we actually get together, we get crazier, which is the mark of true friends. The other night she was at my apartment, and we got giddy adding thousands of dollars of clothes to my imaginary closet. When we discovered our favorite fashion site had a bridal section, we lost it completely. We played a game trying to guess which wedding dresses the other would choose.

Of course we nailed it. We know each other's tastes and closets as well as our own. If there were a Newlywed Game for best friends, we would come away with the dinette set for sure.

Then a lightbulb went off in my head. "Ohmigod, you know what? I've seen the most perfect wedding dress of all time, and it's not in the bridal section. Hang on." I navigated the website with the speed and intensity of a CIA operative.

And then I found it. The Dolce & Gabbana Rose-print Silk Mikado Dress. A stunning white silk gown with gorgeous pink roses painted on the skirt.

My friend gasped. We both needed a moment to recover from its loveliness.

But the price tag?

$14,400.

To reiterate: I am not engaged, not rich, and I don't think my credit card limit goes that high.

But as we basked in the celestial glow emanating from the computer screen, my friend touched my shoulder. "I'm just gonna say it. If you bought this right now, I'd support you, and I'd never tell a soul."

Now that's friendship.

It's also insane. I got us safely away from the computer, but my bff/enabler continued to make her case as we walked my dog outside.

"Maybe you could just order it, and we could try it on in your bedroom, and then you could return it," she said. "After we take pictures, obviously."

I laughed. "I should get my hair done for it."

"Yes! You will get a blow out, and we'll take pictures in it."

We've had a lot of Lucy and Ethel schemes in our time, but this was definitely the worst. "What if something happens to it?"

"Like what? They have free returns!"

"But what if it tears? What if I take it out and it's defective, but they don't believe me? What if I try to send it back and it gets lost in the mail?"

"I'm sure they have a procedure for that."

"Yeah, like charging me fifteen grand that I don't have!"

We took a few steps without talking, our wheels silently turning.

A fellow writer herself, my friend came up with her strongest argument yet. "It'd make a great column."

I didn't buy the dress.

But I did put it on my wish list.

# I Know It When I See It

---

By Lisa

You may have heard that pictures of a topless Kate Middleton were published on the Internet.

Did you look at them?

Fess up.

I looked.

You might think I'm a perv, but I admit, I was curious.

So what do Kate Middleton's breasts look like?

I can tell you exactly.

They're round, and each one has a nipple.

Just like my breasts, and most breasts you've ever seen.

Okay, maybe not my breasts, of late.

Late being since I turned thirty.

Which was when my breasts turned sixty.

I cannot explain why my breasts became a senior citizen before I did. All I know is that my butt is already on social security.

I'm here to tell you that if my breasts looked like Kate Middleton's breasts, I would not be complaining when they showed up on the Internet. In fact, I would email pictures of my breasts to everyone in sight, until people blocked them as spam, and then I still wouldn't stop.

When I saw Kate Middleton's breasts, I got breast envy.

By the way, no woman I know has penis envy.

Freud was totally wrong about that.

Women envy men's power, paycheck, and ability to take the lid off any jar.

But their penises, men can keep.

Not interested.

I have a tough enough time zipping my jeans.

Of course, I understand why it was an invasion of privacy to show the photos, and why the royal couple is upset.

But the royal pair is great.

It was a French magazine that published the photos first, and an Irish newspaper published them next. And finally the Italians, and being Italian-American, I'm very disappointed.

Why did they let the French get the jump?

What about *la dolce vita* and all that?

After all, Italians practically invented breasts. The proof is any fountain in Italy. The water ain't squirting out of fish mouths.

Who wants to drink anything from a fish?

Perhaps to make up for their tardiness, the Italians intended to publish two hundred photos of Kate Middleton's breasts.

Way to go.

That's four hundred breasts, which is plenty for all of Europe. Its economy may be sagging, but guess what's perky?

Right.

Interestingly, the brouhaha, or brahaha, over the photos of Kate Middleton's breasts occurred in the same week that the U.S. Embassy in Libya was attacked and four of its staff slain, including our Ambassador, Christopher Stevens. I was reading the article about the attack online and was clicking through the photos, when all of a sudden, one was a photo of Ambassador Stevens, murdered.

There was no warning at all.

No NSFW.

Not even a NSFHB. Or, Not Safe For Human Beings.

To me, if photos of murdered people are Safe For Work, I don't want to work there.

There are spoiler alerts for a plot twist in *Breaking Bad,* but there's nothing when something breaks as bad as it gets.

Because, for some reason, it's okay to show murdered people on the Internet, but not royal breasts. For example, one headline read, Kate Middleton Topless Photos Spark Worldwide Outrage.

But Ambassador Stevens's photos didn't even raise an eyebrow.

So I guess we have different definitions about what is obscene.

# Stars and Puppies

By Lisa

Sometimes the stars align, and sometimes they collide.

And sometimes they do both, at once.

We begin when Daughter Francesca and I get invited to speak at the National Book Festival in Washington, D.C., about our previous collection in this series entitled *Meet Me at Emotional Baggage Claim*.

Francesca thought of the title, which is very funny unless you happen to be the emotional baggage.

That would be me.

I don't mind being her emotional baggage. On the contrary, I like being a big heavy thing she totes around, like a guilt backpack. Or something she drags behind her, a steamer trunk of doubts, worries, and strongly held beliefs based on no facts at all.

No mother wants to be a mere roller bag, or worse yet, a fanny pack.

At least not Italian mothers.

We leave it to others to say they don't want to burden their children. We think that's what children are for.

Faulkner had the right idea when he said, "The past isn't dead. It isn't even past."

And the great thing about emotional baggage is that even

when I'm dead, I won't be dead. I hope Francesca will carry me around with her in her head, hearing my voice tell her to put the knives in the dishwasher with the pointy end down, or to run a background check on that guy she just met at the bar.

Half of my advice is good.

The other half is awesome.

So, we get ready to leave for the National Book Festival, though we're both busy on book deadline, and it's tax time, too. Because I'm self-employed, I pay taxes every quarter, which means I start hating my government four times a year, like the change of the seasons except none of them is pretty.

No amount of money I send my country seems to satisfy it, and both candidates for president pay less of a tax rate than I do, which reminds me that my country and my government are two different things. I would do anything for my country, but my government can cook its own dinner.

My kitchen's closed.

Anyway, not only are these two things occurring simultaneously, but then, as it happens, my little dog Peach became pregnant, on a date I fixed up. I bred Peach so I can keep her puppies, because as we know, I need more dogs. One of the many advantages to being a single, middle-aged woman is that nobody's around to save you from your own tomfoolery.

And if they were, I wouldn't listen.

But when I take Peach to the vet for a checkup, we learn that she is expected to deliver early, during the National Book Festival. Of course we feel instantly guilty, worried, and fearful, and we have instant emotional baggage from Peach, which may be the first recorded case of emotional baggage being transferred from dog to human, like a virus that jumps species. Still, we make arrangements to have Peach cared for and hit the road, which is when Francesca turns to me in the car.

"I'm worried," she says.

"Me, too. Poor little doggie."

"Agree, but I'm talking about me. I've never spoken in front of a large group before."

"Yes, you have, at bookstores."

"Not like this," Francesca says, and I realize she's right. We were scheduled to speak twice, in front of a thousand people each time, and in all my worrying about my doggie daughter, I had overlooked my real daughter. So I got my act together, gave her a big hug, and drove her to the Festival, where I sat back while Francesca spoke so astoundingly well that I cried.

Someone said to me, "She's her mother's daughter."

And I said, "Thanks, but she's herself, and she's amazing."

(Because no one gives my daughter emotional baggage but me.)

And when we came home, Peach had given birth to three adorable puppies, all beautiful, healthy, and happy.

It was that kind of weekend.

Stars collided, then aligned. And I got to see my own special

Lisa's shining star, Daughter Francesca, rocks the National Book Festival.

**Puppy pileup**

star shine, bathing me in her light, leaving me blissful and blessed.

There can be no greater pleasure, as a parent, than watching your child come fully into her own, taking all of her God-given talents and putting them to their most perfect use.

That feeling?

It's Mom Heaven.

# Milk Shake

By Lisa Scottoline

Today, we're talking breast-feeding.

Not me, but not by much.

I nursed Daughter Francesca until she was twenty-two.

Just kidding.

But in truth, I did nurse her for a long time, though I will never reveal exactly how long, even herein. I've discussed my gray chin hair, my disappearing pinky toenail, and my nonexistent social life, but that is one secret I will never reveal.

Because then you'll know how creepy I am.

It's society's fault, because it can't be mine. Nursing is a great thing and not creepy at all, but society makes you feel like nursing is sexual, even though that's what breasts are for, not for making Victoria's Secret rich.

Maybe that's Victoria's Secret.

That society is stupid.

In my own defense, they say that breast-feeding makes babies smarter, and I will remind you that Francesca went to Harvard.

My breasts deserve full credit, fifty-fifty.

Although the right one, which is bigger, likes to claim 75 percent.

She's so bitchy.

So you learned something today. If you want your kid to get into a good college, grab your breast and get busy.

Hide the car keys, so your kid can't get away.

But this isn't about my breasts, it's about my dog Peach's, who has ten breasts for only three puppies, all of whom are going to MIT because they nurse constantly.

Got milk?

Hell, yes.

Peach gave birth to her puppies about two weeks ago, and I moved them all, plus my desk and my computer, into the bedroom, so I could babysit while I work. Believe it or not, I'm getting more work done than I thought, between cooing over puppies, kissing puppies, taking pictures of puppies, posting pictures of puppies online, then responding to comments about puppies.

The operative word is awwwww.

I feel blissful in my canine maternity cocoon, as blissful as I felt a long time ago in my human maternity cocoon, which is basically the same thing, but for the sitz bath.

Ladies, you know what I'm talking about.

Men, you don't know what I'm talking about, and count yourself lucky. Women have all sorts of equality these days, which is wonderful, but we're still the ones who become besties with the doughnut pillow.

You can thank us anytime.

In fact, there are plenty of similarities between puppy infancy and baby infancy, and I feel the exact same way that I used to. I hang in the same room all day long in sweatpants, never leave the house, and don't have time for a shower.

Okay, the puppies are an excuse. I'm a writer on deadline. Welcome to my world.

Also I haven't slept through the night in forever, because the puppies haven't. They nurse around the clock, slurping and sucking, whimpering and whining, and last night, they even started barking while they nursed.

Francesca never tried anything like that.

But she came close.

Every mother can tell you a story about the time their baby bit them while they were nursing, and I have mine. Francesca didn't really bite, but she did try a nibble.

A nipple nibble.

Or a nip clip.

Mother and baby

The parenting books advise new moms that if you get bitten, you're supposed to say a simple, but firm, "no."

Like a puppy.

But you're not supposed to shame the baby or hit them with a rolled-up newspaper.

In my case, I went with the simple, but firm, "owwwwww."

Plus a rather lengthy, yet creative, string of profanity.

Yet I'm to be forgiven, because at the time, Francesca had a full set of choppers. This would be an occupational hazard of moms who nurse long term.

Dentition.

If you're still nursing by the time your baby has braces, you're on your own.

Even I draw the line.

And at the end of this sleepy but blissful cocooning period, just like before, I'll end up with a new baby.

Actually, I get to keep two puppies, all for myself.

So my pets will have pets.

# The True Meaning of Words

By Lisa

I'm good in an emergency, but first I have to know it's an emergency.

With Hurricane Sandy, I didn't.

The first problem was the name.

One of my best friends is named Sandy, and I love that name, so when I heard that Hurricane Sandy was on her way, I wasn't worried. If you want me to worry about a hurricane, name it Satan.

For Hurricane Satan, I'd move the porch furniture.

But for Hurricane Sandy, I didn't even buy a flashlight.

At the time, I was working around the clock to meet my deadline for the next Rosato & Associates book. I had a generator that would keep power to the computer and the refrigerator, which is all any girl needs.

Also I was working beside the puppies, who were in their fifth week of life, so I was encased in a furry cocoon of adorableness.

Hurricane Puppy Breath.

Sandy was due to strike on Monday, but the weekend before, I still wasn't worried, even with all the hurricane reports on

TV. Every time I looked up from the computer, the TV showed red swaths over Pennsylvania, but they looked like gift ribbons, and then the newscaster started talking about spaghetti bands.

Another misnomer.

If you want me to worry about something, don't call it spaghetti. I love spaghetti. Call it something that worries me, like Internal Revenue Service Bands.

Or that I dread:

Tech Support Bands.

The only thing that started to worry me were TV reports about New York City, where Daughter Francesca lives. Increasingly, by Sunday, the TV news showed New York wrapped in tons of red ribbons, and I began to worry about my puppy.

Er, I mean, my daughter.

So I called Francesca, and we talked all Sunday morning because we couldn't decide whether she should come home. Her apartment was downtown near the Hudson River, but it hadn't flooded in the last hurricane. My thinking wasn't clear, either because I was preoccupied with my book, in major denial, or middle-aged in general. At one point, I remember asking her, "But is there really that much water around New York?"

Francesca answered, gently, "Mom, Manhattan is an island. And they call it the Eastern Seaboard for a reason."

But while we were dithering, Mayor Bloomberg announced that her building was in a mandatory evacuation zone, and she had to evacuate.

Yikes.

So our decision was made for us, but by then, we didn't know how to get Francesca home. I worried about leaving the puppies for that long to go pick her up, and she couldn't take a train, since Amtrak doesn't allow dogs, even in a proper carrier.

Yes, dogs rule our lives.

But we'll blame Amtrak, for being anti-canine.

In fact, let's add Amtrak to our spaghetti bands list. After all, they call it the Northeast Corridor and there's no corridor.

The point is, words have meaning, people. Especially in an emergency.

But as luck would have it, my best friend Franca was in New York that Sunday, running in a race with her daughter Jessica, because that's the kind of cool girls they are. Franca generously offered to pick up Francesca and bring her home, and I took her up on her offer, so Francesca arrived home in a driving rainstorm Sunday night.

In the nick of time.

We lost power an hour later, and for the next four days, but we could rely on the generator until it ran out of propane. We had no Internet, TV, or phone, so we were cut off from the world, like an involuntary writer's retreat. We worked and met our deadlines, and when the power returned, we switched on the TV and learned how very lucky we had been, and how many people were suffering in New Jersey, New York, Delaware, and so many other places, having lost their possessions, homes, and businesses, and some even their lives.

But we also saw police, firefighters, EMTs, the National Guard, and neighbors helping each other, and we talked about how lucky we were in Franca, who had gone so far out of her way to bring Francesca home.

And we thought about the true meaning of words. Not words like Eastern Seaboard or corridor, but words like friendship, gratitude, and love.

Thank you, Franca, for being such an amazing friend.

Lisa and BFF Franca having fun at a 3D movie.

And thank you to everyone who has gone out of his way to help someone in need because of Hurricane Sandy.

You're all invited over.

For spaghetti.

# Rolling Without Homies

By Francesca

You can't feel yourself grow up, but every so often something happens to show you a change has occurred. This is about one of those times.

I live near the Hudson River, a great place to go running, if you like that sort of thing. I don't. I make myself run to stay in shape, but I hate it. It was on a recent slog—I mean, jog—that I noticed people zipping by me on Rollerblades. I loved rollerblading when I was a kid, but I thought the sport had gone extinct in the nineties. Now seeing these people glide by with the wind in their hair, I felt jealous.

So I flirted with the idea of getting Rollerblades but felt too self-conscious to actually do it. My indecision became a running joke between me and my boyfriend, and we were kidding about it at a party, when a tall, beautiful girl overheard us.

"Ohmigod, do people still Rollerblade?" she asked, her glossed lips sneering.

"I know, I know," I said. "But, why not? They're a good workout, they seem fun, and even if they don't look cool, as a woman, don't you get tired of having to work it all the time?"

"*I don't* have to work it," she said, as to leave no doubt that

*I do.* Meanwhile, she was wearing five-inch platform heels, a skintight dress, false lashes, and color contact lenses.

I guess irony didn't go with her outfit.

This mean-girl's input was just the push I needed. As soon as I got home that night, I went online and purchased a pair of inline skates.

In the absence of courage, defiance will suffice.

My mother was supportive, provided that I purchase bubble-boy levels of protective gear. She encouraged me to join a club so I'd have people to skate with, but that seemed like a hassle. I emailed a few friends to persuade them to get Rollerblades, too, to no avail.

Still, I was giddy with anticipation. I tracked the delivery of my new toy from UPS Santa daily. When the skates arrived, I didn't care that I had yet to recruit a single friend; I went out on them that day.

I'm not going to lie, I sucked at first. My street runs downhill to a major road, so I clung to the fence of the neighboring buildings, feeling my way along the hedges and tree boxes. Waiting to cross the street, I held on to streetlights and stop signs like my life depended on it—because it did. And more than once I willfully wiped out to avoid rolling into oncoming traffic.

But soon I got the hang of it, and it was a blast. I saw the sun shimmering over the Hudson, I found the best view of the Statue of Liberty, and I even got some tips from the expert trick-skaters who hang out in Battery Park.

And the few times I did fall, there was always a handsome runner to make sure I was okay. Is this what they mean by a "runner's high?"

Coming home from my solo ride, I ran—or rolled—into one of my neighbors, a young woman who I recognized but hadn't met. Turned out she had a pair of Rollerblades in her closet, and within minutes we made plans to go out together later that week. She's since become a new friend.

Yay!

If my other pals had been reluctant before, my newfound enthusiasm convinced them to go ahead and get skates of their own, marking my first time as a trendsetter.

Who knew?

And although I'm happy to have company, I'm even happier to find that I can enjoy something alone. I surprised myself to learn that I didn't need any validation to try something new, even something I wasn't particularly good at. Being alone is a skill. Having fun alone is empowering.

After all, a grown woman doesn't need anyone's approval to have fun like a kid.

# Happy Thanksgiving

---

### By Lisa

I just saw on the TV news that women are getting their toes cut off to fit into high heels.

Great idea!

I'm wondering if I should cut off my butt to fit into my jeans.

This being Thanksgiving weekend, after turkey, stuffing, and pie, you might be thinking the same thing.

In fact, I bet you are. You probably woke up wondering, what can I hack off to fit into something I don't wear?

So don't put away that carving knife.

Put it to good use!

I'm still trying to imagine how you carve out a waist. Maybe like a blazer? Take a little off the sides?

By the way, I'm not making this up. I saw it on an actual news report, that women are getting their toes cut off or shortened to fit into sexy shoes. When I watched it on TV, I remembered I'd heard it somewhere before, then I realized that it was in an old-school version of *Cinderella* I used to read to Francesca when she was little, which gave us both nightmares.

It's not a magic slipper, it's a magic clipper.

The TV news report said that most women get centimeters taken off their second toe, which is the common culprit. That,

I couldn't relate to. My second toe is one of my favorites, so I'd never stick it in the guillotine. But my pinky toe is another matter. When I'm barefoot, it looks stuck to my fourth toe, like a clingy friend.

Still I wouldn't cut it off.

It's not ugly, it's needy.

In fact, it's leaving on its own. Each year it gets smaller, and I've gone from having an amazing disappearing toenail to an amazing disappearing toe.

In other words, this little piggy went wee, wee, wee, all the way home.

And never came back.

Wee!

The TV news report said that the women are very happy with their foot operations, and so are their husbands.

This, I don't believe. I give men more credit than that. But if he exists, I'd like to meet the man who wants his wife's toes cut off so she can fit into high heels.

I'd like to introduce him to my carving knife.

I'm not sure which part I'd cut off first.

The choice would be between helping him fit into his pants, or helping him fit into his hat.

And if you ever saw me carve a turkey, you'd know I'm a lousy tailor.

The news report also said that 87 percent of women's foot problems are caused by high heels, and that got me thinking, too.

How can we get that number up?

We're slacking, ladies.

Too many of us aren't trying hard enough to be sexy. Maybe if we cut the peep-toe larger, we could cut off more toes and get more peeps? Or maybe we could just cut off all our toes but one and have one giant toe, which would make the shoe fit perfectly.

Hubba hubba.

I also noticed on the dumb reality TV shows I watch, like *The Real Housewives of Beverly Hills,* that the women wear such high heels that they can't walk around by themselves, but have to hold on to their husbands' hands so they don't fall. To me, this is poetic justice. If you cut off your toes to please your man, he should have to walk you around like a toddler.

Because you cut off your nose to spite your face.

But in the end, I'm not criticizing women for the dumb things they do. I've done plenty of dumb things myself, and I'm thinking especially of my second marriage.

Luckily, there's a carving knife for that, too, and it's called divorce.

And for that, I give thanks.

# Novelistic

———————

By Lisa

Life is like a novel.

You never know when you're gonna get a plot twist.

And you hope the ending is happy, and not a surprise.

I learned this last week, though I have been writing novels for twenty years now, some twenty in all.

I might be slow on the uptake.

We begin with some background, which adds irony, always a good thing in a book. In my old broke days, when I was trying to become a writer, I spent five years being rejected before anybody published me.

Like I said, slow on the uptake.

Even after I was published, I still didn't earn a living wage, worked a day job, and also had a mountain of credit-card debt to pay off, since I essentially lived on credit while trying to become a writer.

Turns out Visa is a passport to a new life, albeit at 21 percent interest, back then.

In any event, during this time, I obviously couldn't afford health insurance, so I didn't have any. And by "this time," I mean ten years.

So for a decade, I prayed that I stayed healthy, because there was no insurance company to rely on if I got sick. Things are no different now, when I have health insurance, but still don't rely on an insurance company if I get sick.

Because I have Personal Choice, which evidently means that, on any given day, my insurance company has a personal choice about whether to insure me.

Guess the answer.

But back to the story.

Amazingly, I only had one serious injury during that decade, a tear to a rotator cuff, occasioned by carrying grocery bags into the house. I knew that it was a rotator-cuff injury because I went to a doctor, on my Visa card, and he diagnosed it, telling me my options were surgery or physical therapy. I couldn't afford surgery, but I could afford a few sessions of physical therapy, where somebody taught me how to strengthen the torn muscle by lifting cans of tomato purée.

Fun for Italians!

Miraculously, this worked, but only after I had moved an entire warehouse full of purée.

Now, fast-forward to the present day. Little Tony has been limping around for about three months, with a torn rotator cuff.

If you didn't know dogs had rotator cuffs, join the club.

The vet tried to treat it with medication, but it didn't work, and so Little Tony went to a doggie orthopedist, which is another thing I didn't know even existed, and he decided Little Tony needed either surgery or physical therapy.

Yes, dogs can have physical therapy.

The day they have talk therapy, we're all in trouble.

(It will be ruff!)

I decided against physical therapy, because God knows if I could find tomato cans tiny enough.

Happily, I could afford to do surgery on Little Tony, so my dog had the operation that I couldn't, way back when. It was supposed to be routine, so I wasn't worried about it, and I was driving Daughter Francesca back to New York when the doggie orthopedist called.

"We have a problem," he began to say, and that's all I needed to hear before I pulled over.

I won't keep you in cheap suspense, and the story has a happy ending.

Little Tony survived and lies snoring at the foot of my bed, on an array of narcotics that would impress Dr. Drew. Long story short, the dog had a bad reaction to the anesthesia, and we almost lost the little man.

And it got me thinking, because I didn't see it coming.

It wasn't anybody's fault, and it wasn't in anybody's control.

It just happened, because anything can happen, and at any time.

Both good, and bad.

And though I think of myself as someone who daily counts her blessings, I took for granted that Little Tony was lucky to have the surgery. It never occurred to me that it could kill him.

But now I know better.

And that's the kind of thing that makes life worth living, and novels worth writing.

And reading.

It was a plot twist of fate.

# Post-Puberty

By Lisa

You may have heard that AARP started a dating site.
Now we're talking.
Get my walker.
And my blood-pressure meds.
Mommy's going shopping.
The site is called, "How About We . . ."
But I'm not sure what they mean by that name.
"How About We . . . Compare Our Cholesterol?"
Or "How About We . . . Have a Cup of Decaf?"
Or "How About We . . . Take a Nice Nap?"
So I went on the AARP website to cruise for menfolk, er, I
mean, to learn more about the organization. The first thing
I noticed was that AARP membership begins at age fifty.
Huh?
AARP stands for American Association of Retired Persons,
but if you live in America, you can't retire at fifty. You can't
retire at a hundred and fifty. I'm thinking that my tombstone
will read, RETIRED . . . FINALLY.
In fact, if you're a man who retired at fifty, I want to meet
you. Maybe you're on "How About We . . . Retire While We
Still Have a Heartbeat?"

In any event, I read through the website, which was full of articles with titles such as, How To Have Sex Without Intercourse.

Fascinating, but I've been doing that for quite some time now.

Sex without intercourse is chocolate cake.

I read the article, but I still wasn't sure what they meant. There were too many euphemisms, presumably because I wasn't old enough to be told the truth.

So I skipped to another article, entitled "Ten Great Cities for Older Singles."

Stop right there.

I'm not an "Older Single."

An "Older Single" is a slice of cheese that's past its expiration date.

I haven't expired yet. I know because I'm still working.

Still, I read on and found good news. According to the article, Philadelphia was the eighth greatest city for us older singles.

Wahoo!

The article suggested that "icebreaking opportunities for first dates" include a trip to Independence Hall.

What an idea!

When it comes to the forefathers, who doesn't think foreplay?

The article also suggested a first date to the Philadelphia Zoo.

Another spot that spells romance!

Who hasn't felt primal at the Primate House?

But of course, the more I read through the AARP website, the more I actually began to find articles that interested me, even though I'm not retired. I started to think that maybe I should join AARP. It felt fraudulent, since I'm not retired, but that seemed kinda technical. And two friends of mine, both my age, joined, and they got discounts at the movies.

I clicked through to the membership page, which said it cost sixteen bucks a year to join, which was cheap enough. I would have saved money if I joined for five years, but by this point

I was feeling so old that green bananas were off my shopping list.

Still, I couldn't decide whether to join.

I felt ambivalent about classifying myself as Officially Old.

I told myself, I may be middle-aged, but I'm not aged.

And after all, Mother Mary is an AARP member. Would I really want to join a club that would have us both?

But that may be a different question.

Just when I was mulling this over, an email request came in from my book publicist to go on RLTV, a channel that I'd never heard of. So I went online and found out that it was Retirement Living Television.

Me? Fresh cheddar that I am?

It's a funny thing.

Puberty is a line that's clearly delineated. Your breasts pop.

But how about old age? Your breasts drop?

Enough said.

I went online to the RLTV website, which had photos of people I admire, like Jane Pauley and Bob Vila. Neither of them are retired, but they're still cool, even though they're as old as I am, or even older.

Except that the website did have an article on "Benjamin Franklin—Science Superstar."

Yikes.

But still, that kind of thinking seemed mean-spirited and wrong.

So I joined AARP.

I love being my age, and I've learned that age is arbitrary, anyway. So what if I'm lumped in with sixty-, seventy-, eighty-, and even ninety-year-olds?

I consider myself . . . lucky.

# Gym Rat

---

By Lisa

How many people can say this:

I don't belong to a gym, but my dog does.

Little Tony had shoulder surgery, and now his vet has prescribed rehab for him, or physical therapy.

I had no idea they had physical therapy for dogs, much less that I would open my wallet to pay for it, but I always find the dough for my pets.

I take it out of their clothes budget.

I know I'm not alone, in that I'd spend money on my dog that I wouldn't spend on myself.

Call me crazy.

Or dog-crazy.

My only other choice would be that Little Tony limps the rest of his life, and I couldn't take the guilt.

Also how would he get back to the NBA?

So my dog works out, twice a week. He just had his first session, where he was evaluated and walked on an underwater treadmill. Lucky for me, he didn't need the massage, laser therapy, or acupuncture. The gym also offers a shampoo and blow-dry, but I didn't get one.

I mean, he didn't.

And on the days he doesn't go to his gym, Little Tony is supposed to work out at home. The gym gave me a list of fifteen exercises that target his "Hindlimbs, Forelimbs, and Core."

Evidently the core is a trouble spot for dogs, too. I'm guessing that sit-ups would improve Little Tony's core, but he doesn't even sit.

Maybe he can just cut out the pizza.

Then he could be Littler Tony.

The exercises for his core also include Cookie Stretches, in which the dog stretches forward to reach a cookie.

I can do those.

I also do Chocolate Cake Stretches.

I'm so fit!

You can imagine how well our first at-home exercise session goes, with Push-Ups. In case you were wondering, a doggie push-up is accomplished thusly: "Ask pet to go from the lying position into a sit position and back to the lying position. Ask for 4–6 reps, 2–3x a day, 3–5 days a week."

I asked Little Tony, but he didn't answer.

Then I figured the way to get him to do his first push-up was to bribe him with treats, but all he did was lunge for the treats for five reps.

Pushing up or down was not involved. Only whimpering and whining, which does nothing to strengthen your core.

I should know.

So we moved on to Side Crunches, which are allegedly accomplished like this: "Put a treat on pet's shoulder, hip, and hock, to allow stretching in the neck and back."

First problem, I don't know what a hock is, but no worries, I got my hands full with hips and shoulders. I put the treat on Little Tony's back, but it slides off, whereupon he whips around and gobbles it off the floor.

The only thing that crunches are the treats.

Then I try to hold it on his back, but he keeps moving, turning around in a circle so he doesn't have to do the crunch.

Who can blame him? Not me.

We try the Wheel Barrow, in which I'm supposed to "lift pet's legs and ask pet to move forwards, backwards, and sideways in this position."

I pick up Little Tony's back legs and wheel-barrow him around the kitchen, whereupon he moves forwards, backwards, and sideways—all at the same time.

Until he gets free and runs away.

For five reps.

You get the idea. We struggle through Weight Shifting, Snoopies, and Stair-Lovin', which is when we learn that Little Tony doesn't love stairs.

**Little Tony does his exercises.**

Who does?

Five exercises later, I gain a new respect for Little Tony's native intelligence, and I am puffing and panting.

So one of us got plenty of exercise.

# Gifts for Him

---

By Francesca

It's my first Christmas with my boyfriend, and choosing a gift for him is impossible. We've all heard the lament, what do you get the man who has everything? Well, my boyfriend is the man who needs everything.

He's a musician and travels frequently. He'd be happy with his guitar and whatever clothes fit in a backpack. He doesn't think much of material possessions.

Doesn't he know the true meaning of Christmas?

I've heard him say he needs basics, like T-shirts, but if I get him a pack of Hanes, I'll feel like his mom.

And while a man can give a woman lingerie, I can't bring myself to present my boyfriend with "manties."

I could splurge and get him some designer shirt, but that's not his thing. He's stylish, but not flashy. I actually like how he dresses. I don't want to change him.

Don't I know the true meaning of a relationship?

My girlfriends are easy to shop for because I can get them accessories—costume jewelry, a clutch purse, a hair straightener, the latest wonder mascara. We girls love *accoutrements*.

My boyfriend doesn't even wear a watch, and he wouldn't be caught dead wearing man-jewelry.

Sorry, Mother Mary, he's not Italian.

A friend suggested I get him nice shaving cream, but my boyfriend doesn't shave. His scruff ranges from grizzled to Gorton's Fisherman.

Overpriced bath and body products are a nice girlfriendy gift, but I think they'd be lost on my boyfriend. He's more of a Shampoo + Conditioner in One type. One time he was showering at my place and called out, "Is it okay if I use this Kiehl's shampoo? I don't want to use your nice stuff."

Except that the Kiehl's is dog shampoo. Pip comes before everyone. I buy my shampoo at CVS.

I tried looking online for inspiration, but that was a bust. I used to envy the "Gifts for Him" tab on websites when I had no Him. But now that I do, it turns out those gift lists don't suit Him at all—my boyfriend, I mean.

They probably don't suit Him either, but that's only because He *is* the true meaning of Christmas.

For example, Brookstone recommends wireless TV headphones with a picture of a woman asleep on her man's chest while he looks past her and watches television.

This holiday season, tell your loved one, "I know we're over each other, just keep the volume down."

The Sharper Image suggests an electric nose-and-ear-hair trimmer.

I don't think we're "there" yet.

A site called ThinkGeek.com, which advertises gifts for "Smart Masses," features a hammer with a bottle opener on the back—because drinking while wielding heavy tools is a really "smart" idea.

The stakes are higher when choosing a gift for a significant other than for a friend. A gift for a friend needs only to say: I thought you might like this. A gift for a boyfriend needs to say: I *get* you.

And if I get you the wrong gift, I don't get you.

In my case, my boyfriend is so nice, if I got him something he didn't like, he'd probably pretend to like it, which is even worse.

No faking.

We've been together long enough that we're comfortable, but not so long that we're done trying to impress each other. I still get dolled up to see him.

He has about another six months on that.

So I just want to give him a gift that is fun and cool, maybe a little sexy, but something useful, with a clever twist. I want to give him something that he wants now and that he'll cherish for a long time.

Wait, are we still talking about gifts?

# Mother Mary and the 600 Thread Count

## By Lisa

Mother Mary and bed linens have a long and storied history.

A few years ago, she refused to use the sheets that Brother Frank bought her, because there were bats printed on the fitted sheet and a life-size Batman on the flat sheet.

Mother Mary couldn't picture Batman lying on top of her.

Neither can I.

Visualize amongst yourselves.

Frank had gotten the sheets because they were on sale, which gives you an idea of how the Flying Scottolines roll. If there's a sale, we're buying. Even if it's in the kid's department and Mother Mary has aged out, at eighty-eight.

So I should have expected trouble when for Christmas, Mother Mary asked for new sheets. But I didn't see it coming, and neither will you.

"No problem," said I. "What color do you want?"

(By the way, what a sport I am, huh? Why spring for jewelry when your mother wants sheets? Nothing says love like percale.

After all, it's not like you only get one mother.

Oh, wait.)

But Mother Mary answered, "I want sheets, but I want to buy them myself. Just send me a check, and I'll go to Anna's."

"What's Anna's?"

"The store on the corner."

I shouldn't have asked. Mother Mary loves stores-on-the-corner. She grew up in South Philly, going to the corner grocery, bakery, and butcher. There are precious few stores-on-the-corner these days, but Mom always finds the mom-and-pop stores.

So I send the check and call her a week later. "Ma, did you get your sheets?"

"No, Frank did, and I hate them. They're too big."

"What size are they?"

"600 count."

"Mom, the count of the sheets isn't the size. It's the quality of the cotton."

"These aren't cotton. They're polyester."

Now I'm really confused. "600 count polyester? That can't be right."

"I agree, they're not right. I hate them."

I cut to the chase. "I have an idea. How about I send you a new set of sheets. You have a queen-size bed. What color do you want?"

"White. Cotton. I don't care about the count. I can count."

Gotcha.

"Also, they can't have bugs."

I blink. "Got it, no bugs. Good thing you mentioned that, because I was going to buy sheets with bugs. But now, no way."

"Don't make fun. Your sheets at your house had a bug and that's why my ass itches."

"What?" I ask, thrown for a loop by the non sequitors. You have to roll with the punches when you talk to Mother Mary. Sentences come out of nowhere, like a conversational video game.

"I got a bite on my ass from your sheets."

It makes no sense. The last time she was at my house was during the summer. "Your butt still can't itch from six months ago."

All she says is, "What can I tell you? It was a helluva bug."

So I hang up, go online, find a set of nice cotton sheets, and send them down to Miami, then call a week later. "Ma, how do you like the sheets?"

"I don't."

"Why not?"

"They're not white. I said white."

I cringe. Actually she's right. They were cream, not white, but the ones I liked the most were cream, and I didn't think it would make a difference. "Does it really matter, Ma?"

"Yes."

"Why?"

"On white, I can see the bugs better."

Of course.

And for her birthday, she's getting jewelry.

# The Season of Giving

By Lisa

The good news is that somebody's having fun during the holidays.

The bad news is that it's not exactly under the tree.

It's in the brothels.

Love is all around.

Or to be accurate, in Nevada, where prostitution is legal.

I say this because I just read a newspaper story that the owner of the Mustang Ranch, a brothel near Reno, has been elected to his County Board of Commissioners.

I have no problem with this. I think he's perfectly qualified to be a politician.

I hope he runs for national office. We need more brothel owners in Congress. At least they'd know how to run the House.

By way of background, you might be interested to know who sold the Mustang Ranch to its current owner.

The federal government.

The government had seized it from its former owner because he didn't pay his taxes. Because our government is perfectly fine not only with taxing the income from brothels, but buying and selling brothels.

Uncle Sam be a pimp.

In any event, I'm relieved that, despite the recession, people are still able to buy the necessities.

Evidently, not everybody is tightening his belt.

On the contrary.

And this could be good news for the real-estate market, too. It may be tough to sell a three-bedroom, but if you have a twenty-seven bedroom, you're in luck.

They used to say that the kitchen and the bathrooms sold the house. They were wrong.

In the newspaper story, there was a photo of the Mustang Ranch, and a fair number of the bedrooms had silver poles. I'm guessing this was for fire emergencies.

By the way, there are no mustangs at the Mustang Ranch.

No self-respecting mustang would be caught dead at the Mustang Ranch. A mustang can get a date without cash.

You know why?

Have you ever *seen* a mustang?

To be honest, I haven't either, but I have a pony and an imagination.

Enough said.

Truth to tell, it's probably just marketing to call it the Mustang Ranch. Because there's no sizzle to Middle-Manager Ranch.

In fact, I bet it's not even a real ranch. You shouldn't be able to call it a ranch if the only things that get tied up are the people.

Cattle everywhere should protest.

It's false advertising.

The reason the brothel owner was elected commissioner was because business is booming at the Mustang Ranch, and he has become an economic force in the county.

Wow. I'm proud that America has some growth industries.

I was also happy to learn from the article that there's a Nevada

Brothel Owners Association. I'm just wondering where they go for their convention.

The library?

And believe it or not, the Association has a lobbyist, because in our system of government, even the pimps need pimps.

Interestingly, this news story came on the heels of the election, in which a bunch of states legalized marijuana for medical use.

Another step in the right direction.

Who says we can't do anything about health care?

And so many people suffer from joint problems. Now they can fix it with joints.

Why see a doctor when you can see Dr. Feelgood?

Plus health care is so expensive. Why see your money go up in smoke when you can just smoke up?

Plus, it's the holidays, when everyone is supposed to have fun, relax, and eat too much.

Tailor-made for the ganja.

I have no problem with this, either. After all, I drink margaritas for medicinal purposes.

What ails me? After a drink or two, I forget.

I'm cured.

It's a miracle!

A Christmas miracle.

Happy Holidays!

# Happy New Year Dotcom

---

By Lisa

It's the New Year, and as you may know, I don't like to make conventional resolutions, because that requires me to think about how much I suck.

Who needs it?

Too negative.

Instead, every new year, I prefer to make unresolutions. I think about the things I like about myself and resolve to keep doing them.

As in, I resolve to keep kissing my dogs on the lips.

I can't be the only middle-aged woman with puppy breath.

And this year, I have one big unresolution, which is to continue to dream about harebrained schemes to make money.

I know I'm not alone in this, either.

Does Powerball mean anything to you?

Look, I know I'm lucky to have a job, much less one that I love, but that didn't stop me from buying a lottery ticket when the jackpot reached $500 million. Unfortunately, I didn't win, and neither did you.

Or if you did, and you're single, you need to call me.

Powercall me.

I love to dream about winning the lottery. If I won, I don't know if I would quit writing books, but I would sure like the opportunity to find out.

I wonder if it would be The End.

Anyway, I resolve to keep thinking of harebrained schemes to make money, though other people have me beat. I'm talking about the guy I read about, who sold his last name for $45,000.

His name was Jason Sadler, and he auctioned off his last name to a company named Headsets.com, so he's going to change his name to Jason HeadsetsDotCom.

That's a good ideaDotCom.

Why didn't I think of thatDotCom?

Scottoline isn't that great a name, and for that kind of money, I would change my last name to SomethingDotCom. After all, lots of women change their last names when they get married. Why buy the cow when you get the DotCom for free?

I was going to change my name to Lisa Clooney, if you-know-who called, but now I moved on to Mrs. Bradley Cooper, because for him I would give up my first and last names, without charging a dime.

I'm a bargain!

Then I read about another guy who tattooed Mitt Romney's name on his face and got paid $15,000.

Another great harebrained scheme to make money!

I could start tattooing names on parts of my body, and lucky for me, I have a lot of body.

My butt alone could contain several pages of the phone book.

Maybe I could tattoo my headsets?

Then there was yet another harebrained scheme I read about, where somebody stole $18 million worth of maple syrup from a maple-syrup cartel in Quebec.

First off, who knew there was such a thing as a maple-syrup cartel?

And who's the kingpin, Mrs. Butterworth?

And where do they keep it, a Log Cabin?

I heard they arrested Aunt Jemima.

I'm guessing their hangout is International House of Pancakes.

The police caught them right away, probably because their fingers were sticky.

Whoever they are, my hat's off to them. They didn't kill anybody to take the syrup, and to me, the only thing worth stealing is carbohydrates.

In fact, if somebody hijacks chocolate cake from a chocolate-cake cartel, cover for me.

Of course, the news is full of harebrained schemes to get money, and the biggest dreamer of all is the federal government, because it's currently driving us over the fiscal cliff.

Maybe we could tattoo the members of Congress?

Or maybe just their body parts.

You know which part.

But we'd have to find it first.

Happy New Year!

# Being Good in the New Year

---

By Francesca

I was gleefully naughty this holiday season—like Santa, I assumed any unattended Christmas cookie was meant for me and ate them all. But now it's a new year and I am full of good intentions.

You remember what they say about good intentions.

My girlfriend and I wanted to start off on the right foot, so on New Year's Day, before we went to a movie, we decided to get dinner at a popular vegetarian restaurant in the East Village. We took a seat at a tree-stump tabletop and opened a menu with as many folds as a road map, including a back page labeled "glossary."

In retrospect, this was the first red flag.

But we are young. To us, red flags are life's accessories, like a cute scarf.

The second warning sign, also unheeded, was the group of ballerinas who were seated after us.

"How did you know they were ballerinas?" my boyfriend interrupted, when I was telling him the story later. "Did they walk in so gracefully?"

"No, they were starved and limping."

My friend and I were starving as well, so we didn't waste

time trying to decode the menu. As soon as the waiter came over, we gave our order. My friend chose cauliflower soup and a vegan "Reuben" sandwich, and I decided on the seitan special, whatever that is.

"Would you like any basics?" the waiter asked me. He was tall and thin, with his hair buzzed on the sides and fluffy curls at the top, like a human bean sprout.

"Basics?"

He sighed. "Basics are sides of vegetables to add to your dish."

"What do you recommend?"

"Definitely the sea vegetables."

My brain immediately jumped to the image of a sea cucumber, which I'm pretty sure is a giant slug. "Um, maybe I'll go with the kale."

"It's and/or, so I'll put you down for two orders of kale."

"I have to get two?"

"It's and/or," he repeated, as if this explained everything. "So you can get kale and kale, kale or something else, or kale and something else. And/or."

Pretzel logic, gluten-free.

I opted for the kale AND lentils.

After what felt like forever, our food finally arrived. My friend received a cup of soup and a half-Reuben the size of a tea sandwich. I got a dish with a wet pile of steamed greens and brown beans.

"That sandwich looks small," I said, squinting to see it better.

"Yeah," my friend answered. "Yours looks . . . healthy."

She ate her tiny food in roughly four bites, I ended up pouring balsamic vinegar on mine to make it more palatable. We wanted to be good, but even good girls have their limit. We snagged the attention of our waiter.

"Could I get the other half of this sandwich?" my friend asked sweetly.

"I'm sorry, we can't do that," said the waiter.

I couldn't help myself. "Seriously?"

"Well, I'll have to check with our kitchen," he said.

"Also, I know you guys are busy, but is my entrée coming soon?"

"Did you order something else?" he asked, now looking like a surprised bean sprout.

"Yes, I ordered the special. These were just the basics."

Francesca's a woman, not a rabbit! (The ears are fake.)

He looked at me blankly.

It was and/or, I wanted to cry!

"Let me see what we can do." It was like he had never en-countered two women so hungry. Like we were the Hungry Hungry Hippos, gobbling all the soybeans he could shoot at us.

By the time the waiter rustled up some more spartan food for us, we had to leave to make the movie. We paid—"Sorry, cash only"—and escaped.

At the movie theater, we approached the snack counter. I glanced over my shoulder, in case the ballerinas were behind us again.

"Should we get candy?" my friend asked.

We looked at each other.

I got the Raisinets, it has antioxidants. She got an Almond Joy, it has nuts.

For now, that would be good enough.

# They Call Alabama the Crimson Tide

Spontaneity is a great thing.

But not for Mother Mary.

You would think I would have known this by now, but in fact, I didn't learn it until Daughter Francesca and I went for an impromptu visit.

Which was too impromptu.

It all started back on New Year's Eve, when I called Mother Mary at midnight, as we do every year. God knows when we started this practice, but I've been doing it for several marriages, no matter where I am or what I'm doing on New Year's Eve. To be real, I'm never doing anything on New Year's Eve, so calling my mother is the highlight of the night.

So during our most recent conversation, we wished each other a Happy New Year, but then Mother Mary says something she never says: "I miss you."

I thought I had the wrong number.

My mother and I love each other, but it's not always smooth sailing twenty-four/seven, and I'm trying to figure out exactly what about our fights she misses.

Still, I say reflexively, "I miss you, too," but after we hang up, I realize that I actually do miss her. And it being New

Year's Eve and all, I get a little misty. My remaining drops of estrogen leak from my eyes, and I begin to wonder how many years I have left to fight with my mother.

Because I could go any day now.

So by the end of the week, I'm calling Francesca, then some airlines and hotels, and the very next weekend, we're booked on a plane to Miami to visit Mother Mary. Of course, when you book a flight that late, the only seats available are in first class, but I can work with that. It's nice to have a treat once in a while, and I have only one mother to fight with.

Also it turns out that the only hotel available is crazy expensive, and I stay there only on book tour, when my beloved publisher is paying. But then again, the visit is spontaneous, so beggars can't be choosers. Never mind that I'd be the only beggar at this swanky hotel, but I can work with that, too, because you-know-who deserves it.

That would be me.

I deserve it.

But Francesca is surprised. "Mom, that's not where we usually stay."

"No," I tell her, "but it goes to show how much we love Mother Mary, that we'll force ourselves to fly first-class and stay in a fancy hotel, all for her."

Francesca's eyes narrow. She wasn't born yesterday, nor was my mother, who freaks out when I call to tell her about our upcoming visit.

"You're staying *where*?" she explodes, incredulous. And then she adds, "Why are you coming down anyway?"

I blink. "Because you said you miss me."

"Oh hell," she mutters, but doesn't elaborate.

Fast-forward to Friday night, when Francesca and I are checking in to the swanky hotel, knee-deep in a crowd of cranky travelers. I slide my credit card across the desk, which is when the clerk slides back a form that shows the room rate increasing a third on Saturday night then doubling on Sunday night.

I look up from the form. "You're kidding, right?"

The desk clerk lifts an eyebrow. "Pardon?"

"I understand that the rate increases a little over the weekend, but it costs *twice* as much on Sunday night?"

"Yes," the clerk answers, simply.

Francesca snorts. "What, does the room get bigger?"

Proud of her, I nod. "Yeah, does it turn into Versailles? Or do I just own it outright?"

Nobody laughs except Francesca and me. The travelers behind us begin to grumble, and I feel too embarrassed to ask any more questions, much less refuse to pay, and I know there are no other hotels available anyway. Then I look around and realize that everyone else is wearing either red or green, which I had thought was a nice holiday touch, but the mood isn't Christmass-y at all. In fact, it's downright hostile.

It's only later that I learn that my spontaneous visit is on the weekend of the Orange Bowl, and the hotel is raising its rates because the big game is on Monday night. All weekend, Miami is overrun with battling Alabama and Notre Dame fans, and after a few dinners with Mother Mary and Brother Frank, I learn that the Fightin' Irish have nothing on the Fightin' Italians.

Still Francesca and I had fun, and so did Mother Mary and Frank, so we're glad we went.

But we're glad we're home, too.

Roll, Tide.

# Unreal Estate

———————

By Lisa

I have an old house, which I love.

And hate.

I'm one of those people who says I love old houses.

But I lie.

I'm beginning to accept the truth, which is:

Old houses are a pain in the back porch.

This realization strikes me every year when the weather turns cold. My house has stone walls that are incredibly thick, which means that come October, it's freezing inside. Today it was seventy degrees outside, and fifty in my house.

So you say, turn on the heat, right?

I can't.

Because my house has radiators, which hiss, clang, and bang. I can't hear myself think when the heat is on. If you talk to me on the phone when I have the heat on, you'd think someone is breaking and entering.

So I heat my house by hot flashes.

That's the only way you can live in an old house. If you *are* an old house.

By the way, it's no more habitable in summer, when the

weather turns warm. I can't open any windows, because their sashes are broken.

Yes, my windows have sashes.

Don't ask me why or even what that is. My windows are from an era when dresses had sashes, and I guess they went sash-crazy.

Luckily, my door doesn't have a corset.

But it's hung at an angle, like all the doors in the house. Either the doors have shifted or the floors have, but there isn't a right angle to be found in the house. When you walk around my house, you feel drunk. And if you're drunk when you walk around my house, you're in deep trouble.

After a margarita, I need a designated driver to get to my bedroom.

How did I get myself into this mess, er . . . I mean, old house?

Let's talk turkey.

I always thought that the world divided into two groups: people who like New Construction and people who like Old Houses. It's like Democrats and Republicans, except the disagreement is over something that really matters.

Like an attached garage.

Furthermore, to be perfectly honest, I always sensed hostility between the New Construction people and the Old House people.

Each thinks the other is a snob.

The Old House people look down on the New Construction people as not being classy, as if it's more high-rent to have heating you can hear.

And the New Construction people look down on the Old House people as being dirty, because they prefer what's essentially a Used House.

It's like New Construction people think that Old House

people are filthy, and Old House people revel in their colonial filth.

To be fair, all of this could simply be PTSD from my second marriage. Thing Two was an Old House person, and I was a New Construction person, albeit secretly. I kept my preference to myself, as I sensed it wasn't as ritzy, so when we looked at old houses, I fawned over the deep windowsills that would look so great with a windowseat, which I would never use, as I'm not a cat.

All I really wanted was a family room.

Because in an Old House, there's no place for the family to be, except around the hearth.

Where's the hearth? Take a right at the butter churn. Don't trip over the spinning wheel.

So of course, my second marriage being the picnic that it was, we ended up with an Old House and no family room. I lived in my Old House for years until I subtracted a husband and added a family room.

Yay!

My solution since then has been to take my Old House and constantly remodel it, thus changing it into New Construction.

Or Old Construction.

Like me.

# I Want a Name When I Lose

---

By Lisa

Weeks later, I'm still recovering from my visit with my mother.

She's Earthquake Mary.

And I'm having aftershocks.

I have written about how love and worry bind Mother Mary and me, in that she and I always worried about Francesca, when she was a baby. Well, times have changed, and now Francesca and I are worried about Mother Mary.

Why?

No reason, aside from the fact that she's eighty-nine and alone all day, while my brother is at work. Francesca and I worry that she could fall, or choke on food, or any number of things that Mother Mary and I used to worry about with baby Francesca.

The trip down to Miami only made us more worried. For example, when I was leaving the hotel to go pick up Mother Mary, she called me on the phone. "Help!" she said, her voice trembling.

"What happened, Ma?" My heart started to pound. "What's the matter?"

"I need you!"

I grabbed my purse and headed for the door. "I'm on my way, but what is it? Should I call 911?"

"Don't be silly. I can't change the channel on this damn remote."

Whew.

So I exhaled.

Until I found out that after we hung up, she left the house, went to the next-door neighbor's, and asked him to come over and change the channel for her. That made me worry even more. I told her, "Mom, why didn't you wait until I got here? You could have fallen on the sidewalk."

"I didn't fall."

"But you could have."

"Oh, shut up."

"But I'm worried about you."

Mother Mary waved me off with a frown. "I don't need you to worry about me."

"I can't help it," I tell her, raising my voice. "I love you!"

I don't add, she's the one who taught me that love and worry are the same thing, and the way you show someone you love them is to yell at them.

The more you love, the louder you yell.

That's why if you drive past any house containing Scottolines, you'll hear screaming.

It's not murder, it's love.

We're going deaf BECAUSE WE LOVE EACH OTHER!

Anyway to stay on point, the three of us go out to dinner, but the incident with the remote control occasions the umpteenth version of this conversation:

"Mom, why don't you move up north, with me?"

"No."

"But I'm home all day. We could be home all day together."

"No."

"But, if you had a problem, like with the remote control, you could tell me. You should move up north with me."

"Don't tell me what to do." Mother Mary scowls deeply, which is when I realize we're talking about a different kind of remote control.

In fact, we're having remote control issues.

Mother Mary has the control.

I have the remote.

So I let it be, for this round. I know I'm not the only one trying to come up with the best solution for where an older parent lives, and I'm lucky enough to still have a mother around to worry about.

Or yell at.

So we talk again about her getting a Life Alert, but she says no. Mother Mary doesn't think she needs it and she hates pendants.

I yell, "BUT IT'S NOT ABOUT THE PENDANT!"

"I SAID NO!" Mother Mary yells back.

After our testy dinner, she actually agrees to go to see a movie with Francesca and me, which I suspect is her way of saying I'm sorry for not wanting to live with you.

Works for me.

Francesca reads through the movie listings on her phone, trying to lighten the mood, though I'm cranky and Mother Mary is crankier.

We buy tickets for *Les Misérables* because we are Les Misérables.

We go to the movie and sit down in a little row, three generations of unhappy Scottolines, now with popcorn and Raisinets.

But in time, my mood improves, and so does Mother Mary's. Rapt and teary, we get swept up in the movie, because it's almost as dramatic as we are.

**Three generations of fun**

And at some point, Mother Mary rests her head on my shoulder and falls asleep, like a small child.

I stay as still as possible, so she stays asleep.

The yelling may be over, but the worry abides.

And the love.

# Thought Bubbles

---

By Lisa

You've probably seen the Dove soap commercial in which a forensic artist sketches a woman according to her own description and she looks terrible, and then sketches a second picture of the woman according to a description of her by a stranger, and she looks great.

Who is surprised by this?

Not me.

I could've told you that women are their own worst critics. I also could've told you that forensic drawings make everybody look ugly.

But that's not my point herein.

The tagline of the campaign is, "You Are More Beautiful Than You Think." And everyone is hailing this as a profound way to look at women's self-esteem, or for women to look at their own self-esteem.

I don't agree.

I think it really doesn't matter if you're beautiful or not.

Let's be real.

I don't need a forensic sketch to tell me what I really look like, because I have a mirror. And to tell the truth, every time I look in the mirror, I have the exact opposite reaction:

I thought I looked better than that.

It's not like I have a big ego or think that I'm especially attractive. But I can tell you that when I look in a mirror, it's a disappointment. So I don't even want to think about what would happen if I ran into a forensic sketch artist and he started drawing me. I might take his pencil and stick it where the sun don't shine.

In other words, my own personal tagline should be, "I'm Not As Beautiful As I Think."

But who cares?

I'm not a model.

I'm a writer, a mother, and a fifty-seven-year-old woman. Bottom line, I'm fine with how I look, even though I'm not beautiful.

And all I want from Dove soap is to get me clean.

When did a soap company get to be our national therapist?

I wish Dove would get out of the self-esteem business and figure out how to get me even cleaner, longer. Or how to make soap with more suds, because I like a lot of suds.

Dove, don't flatter me by telling me I'm not only beautiful, but more beautiful than I think. Because I wasn't born yesterday, and I don't look it.

In other words, don't lather me up, just lather me up.

I guarantee we'll never see a soap commercial like that for men. Nobody will ever sell soap by talking about how men are handsomer than they think. In the first place, most men aren't half as handsome as they think, but they don't care.

And they're right.

I like Dove soap, but I don't need it to build my self-image. And I don't want it to do so by telling me that I'm *more* beautiful than I think, because it assumes that beauty is the key to our self-esteem. What should matter to women is who we are and how we act, and if we set our own dreams and fulfill them.

None of that has anything to do with what we look like.

It's what you do, not what you look like, that makes you feel happy and good about yourself.

And even ugly women deserve self-esteem.

Dove might know something about soap, but their analysis—like beauty itself—is only skin deep.

I don't even give them an A for effort. Dove has us worrying about the wrong things. Dove isn't our friend, it's our frenemy.

I think that this is the softest sales job ever.

And you know who's taking a bath?

Women.

# A Dog's Pursuit of the Far-Fetched

By Francesca

When was your last field trip? Was your mom still packing your lunch?

Mine was last Monday, when I convinced my boyfriend and best friend to accompany me to the Westminster Dog Show.

The best part about Westminster during the day is that you can see all the dogs "backstage." Prep areas are designated by breed, and each exhibitor sets up shop differently. One Bichon Frise's station was decorated with a T-shirt with its face and name in air-brush script hung like a banner, like something you'd see in a tribute to Tupac or a prize-winning boxer.

A human boxer, that is.

But here, the dogs were the celebrities, and I was star-struck. We were members of the grubby public, weaving through rows of Pomeranians posing for photos like Kardashians, Yorkies with smoother hair than a supermodel, and greyhounds slim enough to wear sample-size couture.

Their groomers could have a great side business doing people. I want the Silky Terrier Blow-Out for my next party.

At one point, I lost my boyfriend. I used my Terminator-Girlfriend Sight™ to scan the crowd for any girls hoping to give new meaning to "professional handler."

I caught him staring, but not at a woman. He was drop-jawed at the strangest-looking dog I'd ever seen—medium-sized and the color of burnt toast, the dog was completely hairless except for a wiry little Mohawk.

"It's a Xoloitzcuintli!" my boyfriend said. He explained it was an Aztec name for this ancient dog once bred to guard the dead. The handler had been showing Xoloitzcuintlis for seventeen years, which is how long it takes to correctly pronounce the name.

Meanwhile, my best friend was busy snapping pictures and asking questions about certain breeds, ostensibly to help her brother choose a dog back in Boston. But as I watched her coo over a sheepdog, her inquiries began to sound like, "I'm asking for a friend."

I see pet hair in her future.

My dog is a Cavalier King Charles Spaniel, so I was dying to see the Cavalier-breed class. I worried my less-obsessed friends might get bored watching thirty nearly-identical dogs prance around a ring, but they were game. We picked our favorites and placed imaginary bets on the winner. Our judging standards were: cute, really cute, insanely cute, and shiny coat.

Toward the end, one of our favorites got eliminated. But just our luck, the female handler brought her dog right behind us to watch the rest. I couldn't wait to pet the dog, but when I turned around to ask, I saw the woman was upset; her face was flushed and she fought back tears.

I went into comfort mode. "He's beautiful. We all loved him from the start."

"Thanks. He should still be in there," the woman said, crestfallen. "He's so good, he should've gone farther. There are dogs in there that, that—" She shook her head before saying anything unsportsmanlike. "He's just a terrific dog." She held the wiggly pup closer to her chest and softened. "But thank you."

In the end, the winner was chosen, a beautiful dog selected from a group of equally beautiful dogs, but I couldn't get the woman out of my head. It's unusual to see someone so unguarded and emotional. She lost and she was disappointed, angry, sad, the works. She wanted it, she wanted to win, and she wasn't afraid to show it, even in the face of defeat. Her guts and her passion impressed us more than any cup or ribbon.

It made me think of my friends and me. My friend and I want to make a living as authors. My boyfriend wants to be a rock star. We have big dreams, and we're at the stage of our lives where we have the time and freedom to try and make them happen. But we're also of a generation that lives under the hipster ethos that there is nothing worse than caring too much, and it's better to enjoy something ironically than to fess up to wanting something you might not get.

I realized I've never been as bravely open as this woman about wanting something, going for it, and believing I deserve it. Her dog lost and she was taking it hard, but you knew she would be back.

And so would we.

# Fish & Game

---

By Lisa

In most jurisdictions, state law forbids what's going on in my bedroom.

No, not that, silly. I'm not talking the Vice Squad.

I'm talking Animal Control.

Or you could say, *Fifty Shades of Puppy.*

Let me paint you a picture.

On the left side of my bedroom is something called an ex-pen. No, it's not something you put your ex in.

That would be Hell. As in, rot in.

Handcuffs, of course, would be involved, but used for their intended purpose. Whips would be nice, and so would chains.

That's the kind of sex fantasy I have.

Fantasies where bad things happen to people I've had sex with.

But to stay on point, the ex-pen on my left side of the bedroom holds my dog Peach's three puppies, who are predictably adorable and spend their day engaging in a variety of puppylike activities, including peeing and nursing, in a continuous loop.

If you carry a water bottle around with you all day, you know these things are related.

But if you don't carry a water bottle around but are a middle-aged woman, you know these things aren't necessarily related. *Fifty Shades of Gray Hair.*

On the right side of my bedroom sits another ex-pen containing Little Tony, who is still recuperating from shoulder surgery. He's on pain meds, antibiotics, cold compresses, and restricted activity, which means he isn't allowed to run, play, jump, or have any fun for the next three months.

I carry him upstairs and down to take him out to the bathroom, and at this point, I do everything but go to the bathroom for him, though I probably could.

You may recall that he lacks a foreskin.

Coincidentally, so do I.

In between the two ex-pens, I've shoved my desk, a chair, and a computer, because I have a deadline for a new novel. I can't walk around my bedroom, because there's no room left.

By the way, in case you were wondering, Ruby The Crazy Corgi watches this insanity from the threshold to the bedroom, held at bay by a gate. And Spunky the Cat, whom I adopted after my neighbor Harry passed away, is hanging out down the hall in Francesca's bedroom, behind a gate of his own.

Bottom line, we're all on lockdown except my cats Mimi and Vivi, who have complete run of the entire house, both day and night.

Anybody who owns cats will surmise immediately, and probably correctly, that Mimi and Vivi designed this plan.

At night I think I hear them downstairs, laughing and drinking beer.

Still I'm not complaining about any of this, because as it turns out, I'm having the time of my life.

People say I must be getting no work done, but on the contrary, I've written more words, more quickly than I ever have before. A writer's job is to sit in a chair and write, and so I do, except for breaks when I go cuddle something furry.

Freud wondered what women want, but he should've asked me, because the answer is:

Something to cuddle!

And a job!

So I'm hoping I can't be the only person on earth who plans their life this badly and creates this many of their own problems, yet somehow everything turns out not only all right, but awesome.

Surely there has been a time in your life when you shouldn't have been happy, but you were.

**Ruby is banned from the puppy party.**

**Boone enjoys some alone time.**

When everyone thought you were nuts, but you felt the sanest ever?

Because some plot twists are for the better, and some endings are not only happy, but a surprise.

# Recipe for Disaster

---

## By Lisa

Turns out you're never too old to call your mother about a recipe.

And regret it.

We begin when I decide to cook a nice meal for Daughter Francesca, because we're about to start book tour. I decide to make eggplant parm, which I haven't made in years. Mother Mary, as you can guess, is the Queen of Eggplant Parm, and she has the best recipe ever. When I was in my twenties, I used to call her for her recipes because I'd never made the dish. But now, in my fifties, I have to call her because I can't remember if I made the dish or where my keys are or what year it is.

I actually forgot that, yesterday.

At least I think it was yesterday.

Back then, in my twenties, my big question was whether you had to preheat the oven.

Mother Mary always said yes.

So I did, but now I learned that the answer is no.

Preheating the oven is as big a lie as the check is in the mail.

Believe me. Take risks. Don't preheat.

Anyway, I couldn't remember the order of business for breading the eggplant slices, whether it was egg, flour, and bread crumbs, or flour, egg, then bread crumbs. I know it seems obvious, but when I breaded a slice in the logical order—egg, flour, bread crumbs—the eggplant's surface cratered like bad skin.

So I called Mother Mary for the recipe, but before I could ask her my question, she asked me hers: "Did you preheat the oven?"

I paused. "No."

"You have to."

"I will," I lie.

"Don't lie. Do it now."

"Ma, I haven't even made the eggplant yet. If I preheat the oven from now, I'll use up enough energy to bake earth. So tell me, what's the order?"

"Wait. The oven has to be 350 degrees. No more, no less."

"Got it. Now, Ma—"

"Also you have to peel the skin off, did you do that?"

"No. I read that it has vitamins." Also I'm too lazy.

"Wrong! Peel it!"

"Okay, I will," I lie again. "Now, Ma—"

"Did you leave the eggplant slices out overnight, to let the water leak out?"

I fall silent, trying to decide whether to lie a third time.

"You have to do it the night before. You put salt on the slices, lay them flat between two plates, and put your iron on top of the plate, to weigh it down."

I'm still trying to decide how to respond. I remember growing up, I used to wonder about the eggplant slices between two plates, sitting on the counter all night. By the next morning, about half a teaspoon of eggplant water had dripped into the sink.

Like it matters.

So of course I didn't take anything out the night before. I never make a recipe that requires taking anything out the night before. I never think that far behind.

Also I don't own an iron.

Other than that, I followed her recipe exactly.

Mother Mary asks, "Did you drain them last night?"

"Yes," I lie. Third time's a charm.

"You didn't, I can tell," Mother Mary says firmly. "Salt the slices, drain them, and make the parm tomorrow night."

"Ma, tomorrow night I'll be at a book signing." By the way, I could remind her that the book in question, *Meet Me at Emotional Baggage Claim,* is almost entirely stories like this one, about her, but I'm sensing the irony might be lost.

Mother Mary raises her voice, agitated. "Then make the parm the next night."

"Ma, I have to make it tonight. So what's the order—"

"YOU CAN'T MAKE THE PARM IF YOU DIDN'T DRAIN THE EGGPLANT!"

So you know where this is going. Shouting and fighting, ending in false promises, heavy guilt, and mediocre eggplant parm.

In other words, dinner, Scottoline-style!

# Number One Can Be Hazardous to Your Health

By Lisa

I have an embarrassing story to tell you about how I tore my quadriceps muscle.

I didn't do it skiing or running, snowboarding or hiking.

All I did was get off the toilet seat.

Yes, I'm too old to pee-pee without hazard.

Last Sunday I left the bathroom, took a step, and got a pain in my thigh that felt as bad as childbirth without the ice chips.

I tried to take two more steps, but couldn't walk. I broke out in a sweat and cried out in pain. The dogs didn't notice anything amiss. I do the same thing when *Downton Abbey* is over.

I didn't know whether I should go to the hospital or not, so I hopped on one leg to the laptop, logged on to Google, and typed in "my left thigh really really really hurts."

I often whine to Google. Not only is it free, but you don't have to marry and later divorce it, which is decidedly not free.

Anyway, the first thing that came up on my search was: BLOOD CLOT.

Yikes.

That made my decision for me. I was going to the hospital. To a middle-aged woman, BLOOD CLOT is almost as scary a word as BATHING SUIT.

But I didn't know whether to call an ambulance. On the one hand, the hospital is very close to my house, and I could drive there quicker than an ambulance could get to me. Also, I was already two centimeters dilated.

On the other hand, if I waited for an ambulance, I would have time to put on a bra. You may remember that I'd resolved not to be caught dead without a bra in the ER again.

But then I worried about *really* being caught dead.

So I grabbed my keys, hopped and yelped my way to the car, and drove to the hospital, but by the time I found a parking space, I couldn't walk at all and practically fell out of the car. I hopped and yelped to the ER, waving frantically to catch someone's attention through the glass.

Needless to say, this did not work. I pictured myself dying outside the automatic doors and the hospital personnel gathering around, shaking their heads sadly. I could imagine what they'd say:

"This dead woman looks a little like Lisa Scottoline."

"It's definitely Lisa Scottoline. And she's braless again. Yuck!"

"I know! And can you imagine her in a bathing suit?"

Luckily, this did not happen, except in my nightmares. By the way, in my dreams, everybody stands around me and says:

"This dead crone is too hideous to be Lisa Scottoline."

"Agree, and I hear she's a great author."

"She is, and I'm going out right now to buy all of her awesome books!"

"Me, too!"

But back to reality.

I hobbled into the ER, where all manner of caring and competent personnel descended, whisked me into an examining room, connected me to various monitors, and determined that I didn't have a blood clot, but a torn quadriceps muscle.

Apparently, Google didn't go to medical school.

Then they admitted me to the hospital and gave me morphine.

And I'm here to tell you that I like morphine even better than chocolate cake.

If they gave morphine to women in labor, I would become the best Catholic on the planet.

If they gave morphine to the general population, there would be no crime or recession. No one would wear bras or pay bills. Everybody would grow cellulite but they wouldn't care, because they'd know that there are more important things in life.

Like morphine.

In fact, here's what happened to me on morphine: I slept through the season finale of *Downton Abbey,* and when I woke up, I didn't even mind.

But I will tell you a dirty little secret. Morphine is constipating.

Though even that has a bright side.

It keeps you away from those dangerous toilet seats.

# Urban Studies

---

By Francesca

I've been living in the city for four years, so I've earned the equivalent of a bachelor's degree in urban living. I've had all the rites of passage: My apartment's been burglarized, I've had a regular flasher, I've braved the Whole Foods lines after work, I've gone to the beach via train, I've watched the fireworks from a rooftop, and I've eaten pizza standing in the street. They say you have to toughen up to live in a major city, and in a lot of ways, it's true. For every extra convenience, something else is a little harder. And in turn, we get a little harder. For instance, I knew I was a real New Yorker when . . .

My girlfriend and I were leaving a party late on one cold winter's night, and we were desperate to catch a cab home—along with apparently everyone else in New York. The streets were lined with people waiting for a taxi, and each one seemingly on a luckier corner than ours. But the thing about a city is, at any given moment, there are roughly a hundred people wanting to do exactly what you want to do. So we waited, shivering on the sidewalk for a good twenty minutes while we watched occupied cabs fly by with their cozy, smug passengers in the back.

Finally one with its light on came our way and slowed at a

traffic light. We raced over the cobblestones in our heels like mountain goats; this was *our* cab, broken ankles be damned. I lunged for the door and shouted our destination. The cabbie gave a wordless nod, unlocked the doors, and we hopped in.

We'd just buckled our seat belts and breathed a sigh of relief when the cabbie asked me to repeat our destination. I did, but this time he shook his head, and said only, "No."

"No?"

"I'm not going that way, I'm going north."

"It *is* north."

He shrugged. "It's northwest."

"So you won't take us?" my friend asked.

He waved his hand as dismissal.

I groaned, and we got out of the car. I was already looking for the next cab when I heard behind me:

"HEY!" The driver was out of his cab and marching toward me. "Why you gotta slam my door?"

For a second, I was stunned silent. Sure, I was frustrated, but I didn't think I had slammed anything. The cabbie didn't wait for me to respond.

"Why can't you be a lady? Why you gotta slam my door? You gonna break my door."

Had this been my first year in New York, I might have been scared to have an angry man bearing down on me, but it wasn't.

"*Excuse* me?" I said, matching his volume and raising him a whole lotta attitude. " 'Break your door?' Oh, please. I'm a 115-pound woman, I couldn't break your door if I tried!"

It takes a certain composure to both shout at a stranger *and* lie about your weight.

The cab driver retreated, and my friend applauded my chutzpah. I felt like I'd accomplished something in my meanness. I thought I had passed Urban Living 101.

But more recently, something happened that made me think

toughness isn't the central message of city life. I was writing at my desk beside an open window when a giant cement truck just outside leaned on its air horn for a solid forty-five seconds at a parked van blocking its way.

The sound was earsplitting, so I hung out my window fully prepared to unleash some Philly-bred, New York–honed rage, but then the driver looked at me. And in that second of eye contact, I saw all of his frustration, and without thinking, I did something very provincial.

I smiled.

And then *he* smiled.

I put up my hands in the Italian-but-universal gesture for "Whaddyagonnado?" and—get this—we *laughed*. Genuine, tension-relieving laughter. And that laughter blew off more steam than blasting horns or screaming out windows ever could. I've never felt so bonded to a stranger before in my life.

The truck driver proceeded to calmly reverse out of my street, and I gave him a wave good-bye.

Now I wonder if I had been a little nicer to that cabbie, looked him in the eye, told him I didn't mean to slam his door, and explained that we were cold and tired, too, maybe I would've had that ride back home.

# Season to Taste

---

By Lisa

It's good to know that if you can't rely on the federal government, you can always rely on your state government.

I say this because I recently saw a news article that reported a certain state government had enacted a law that permitted its citizens to eat any roadkill they found, without fear of penalty.

Gee, thanks!

If Marie Antoinette said, Let them eat cake, there's always a politician around to say, Let them eat raccoon.

I hasten to point out that the state in question isn't my own, the Commonwealth of Pennsylvania.

Such a silly law would never pass in Pennsylvania.

We don't need a law to tell us it's okay to eat roadkill.

We just dig right in.

Finders keepers, squirrels are weepers.

The lawmakers who passed the bill thought it was a good idea because the roadkill would otherwise be "a waste."

Which is an excellent point.

Mother Mary always taught me that I had to clean my entire plate and also the shoulder of I-95.

Think about the starving people in China the next time you leave a flattened chipmunk in your rearview mirror.

Only a politician would find the merit in not wasting waste.

But be careful. If you eat too much waste, it goes to your waist.

One of the politicians also pointed out that the new law would allow citizens to eat roadkill themselves or they could "legally call the food bank."

Good job!

I'm glad those politicians are preparing for any eventuality. This way, they covered people who'd already eaten their fill of roadkill.

You know the feeling.

When you just can't stuff another dead snake in your mouth.

It's like Thanksgiving.

In Hell.

Leave room for dessert!

And don't hog the groundhog.

It takes a special kind of person to believe that the homeless and jobless should be fed by vermin that BMWs have plowed to smithereens.

And that person is a politician.

Don't you wish you were that smart, or kind?

That's why normal people don't run for office.

We're normal.

We don't like it when our meal comes embossed with zigzags.

And we don't loosen our belts for a steel-belted radial.

The funny thing is that opponents of the law allowing people to eat roadkill objected to its passage because they felt that road-kill might not be a "safe food source."

Now that would be a perfect example of the kind of fine point you have to be a politician to perceive.

Because politicians are always concerned about our safety and welfare, but when it comes to our dignity, we're on our own.

In other words, they're happy to have us crawling along the highway with a spatula, but they envision us sticking a meat thermometer in a possum.

Interestingly, it turns out that the food bank wrote the politicians a letter saying that they would not accept roadkill as food.

Oh, excuse me.

I guess somebody's picky.

Come to think of it, I have a problem with the term "food bank." To me, food should be plentiful and easily available to everyone, especially in a country as great as ours. The only thing that should contain food is a refrigerator.

Banks should contain things that are scarce and hard to get, like money.

Or men who date women over fifty.

Now that would be the kind of bank that would get my account.

But it would be a very small bank.

Very.

Small.

You may have heard the expression that the law is an ass, but I don't agree.

I think the lawmakers are asses.

When they see roadkill, they want us to bring our own fork.

But to them, I say, fork you.

# Airport Insecurity

---

By Lisa

You may have heard about the airline that charges passengers according to how much they weigh, which I think is a great idea.

Because airline travel isn't humiliating enough.

Never mind that when you stand in the security line, you have to undress in front of perfect strangers.

First you take off your shoes, so you can stand there awkwardly in your bare feet. You lose three inches, but you gain ringworm.

Next you have to take off your belt. It is not embarrassing at all to have to lift up your shirt and unfasten your belt, especially if you have to suck in your belly.

Not that I would know.

I have a belly, of course.

I just don't bother sucking it in.

Then you unfasten your belt, and try not to make eye contact with the man in front of you as you slide it slowly through your belt loops.

I've had dates with less sexual chemistry.

Fifty Shades of Delta.

Finally you take off your coat and your sweater, stripping

down to your T-shirt. Nobody throws any dollar bills at you, and there's not even a pole. It's the Terminal A striptease, and believe me, I've seen some of those businessmen in line and I know their wheels are going up.

Next you proceed to the full-body scanner and lift your arms over your head, so the machine projects a life-size image of your bra to everybody in the tristate area.

With some women, it's free porn.

In my case, it's comic relief.

Plus I read recently that some of these machines use X-rays, and all I have to say is, TSA is in deep trouble if my breasts glow in the dark.

Whose side are you on, Marie Curie?

Let's not forget that when you're in the full-body scanner, you have to put your feet in the yellow outlines on the mat. But I'm short, and I can never reach the outlines with my feet. The other day, a TSA guy actually said to me, "Lady, you have to move your legs farther apart."

Dude. No, I don't.

Although I'm a sucker for a man in uniform.

With a big wand.

Besides, I don't think my legs go farther apart, anymore. They like to be close together, all the time. In fact, they might have grown together, so when I travel, I'm a mermaid, with carry-on.

But let's be real, ladies. Which machine is more embarrassing— a full-body scanner or a mammography machine?

How about a show of hands?

Or something else . . .

Obviously, I'm all for airlines charging us by weight. Our self-esteem can be dangerously high at times. So by all means, why not put a big scale right next to the gate? Make sure it has a large, blinking display, so that everybody can read it clearly. Better yet, announce it on the loudspeaker systems.

WELCOME TO PHILADELPHIA. LISA SCOTTOLINE WEIGHS 132 POUNDS. ALSO HER LEGS NO LONGER SEPARATE. SHE MAY EVEN HAVE A HYMEN, WHO KNOWS?

And why stop there, in terms of humiliation? Get an overhead projector and show the world our W-2s.

And by the way, the airline charges overweight baggage at the same rate as the passenger's "personal weight."

Cruel.

You know what I think?

The weight of this old bag is none of your business.

And I feel the same way about my luggage.

# Festival du Crime

by Lisa

Once in a while a crime story comes along that makes you smile.

I'm talking about the jewelry thefts at the Cannes Film Festival, which to me are good, clean fun.

After all, there's no murder or mayhem, which can be icky.

I'm speaking, of course, as a crime writer.

Anyway, to make a long story short, the Cannes Film Festival has a red carpet that cries out for young actresses to swan around in borrowed gowns and glittery diamonds. There was probably a time in the world when this was unusual, but nowadays there are red carpets, young actresses, and glittery diamonds appearing somewhere on a weekly basis, filmed for television shows that no one watches.

Except me.

I will watch diamonds when they're worn by anybody, anyplace, at any time. Yes, I'm that idiot who will actually stand in front of a jewelry-store window at the mall and stare at inanimate objects.

Correction.

Diamonds only appear to be inanimate, but they sparkle, shine, and twinkle, all while sitting in the very same place.

What happened in Cannes was that an employee of Chopard, a Swiss jewelry maker, brought a lot of its diamonds to the film festival to lend to the actresses. He put the diamonds in the safe in his hotel room, only to find out later that somebody had ripped the safe out of the wall and stole the diamonds, worth $1.4 million.

By the way, the police station was located directly across the street from the hotel.

I'm betting the thief was Gregory Peck.

And the detective was the Pink Panther.

And for the record, I was not in Cannes at the time of the heist. Oddly, I wasn't invited to the film festival this year.

Or, well, ever.

At the time, I was home, picking ticks off the dogs.

Talk about glamour!

But I read about the burglary when it happened, trying to decide if I was appalled or admiring. It was a crime that didn't involve blood or forensic analysis, which is a point in its favor. To be fair, the jeweler lost money, but was undoubtedly insured. And the insurance company lost money, but your point is?

To me, anytime an insurance company pays anything, anywhere, it's a victory for all of us.

In fact, I'm pretty sure that insurance payoffs are like cockroaches in reverse, in that every time you see one payment, there are twelve thousand other claims that are being denied.

I'm not even worried about whom the insurance company will pass its costs on to, because the answer is that it's the next person who insures millions of dollars' worth of jewelry.

In other words, not me or you.

As for the young actresses, they undoubtedly got substitute diamonds to wear and the red carpet kept rolling. As far as I can tell, the only loser in the entire scenario was the Chopard employee who thought it was a good idea to entrust $1.4 million worth of diamonds to a hotel-room safe, password-protected by the four digits of his dog's name.

Whoops, I just gave away my diamond-protecting password.

RUBY.

Ironic, no?

But if that wasn't an entertaining enough crime for you, during the same film festival at Cannes a week later, a diamond necklace was stolen during a party, and this time, the gems were worth $2.6 million.

Somebody's improving.

The necklace belonged to another Swiss jeweler, De-Grisogono.

Today, I'm guessing they are DePressed.

I read that the thief got the necklace past eighty bodyguards, local police, and hotel staff.

Somebody's going to lose his job.

They got conned, so they'll get Canned.

# Relationship Spoiler Alert

By Francesca

My boyfriend isn't caught up on *Breaking Bad*. This may not sound like a crisis to you, but it is.

There are only two episodes left in the greatest show on television, and as if that weren't traumatizing enough, the writers are torturing my favorite characters to the bitter end. And I can't say a word to my boyfriend.

No spoilers.

I suffer alone.

We love watching our favorite shows together. But with the advent of DVR and Netflix, watching a show as a couple has gotten complicated.

When it comes to appointment-television, how do you sync your calendars?

First, my boyfriend got me into *Game of Thrones*. He was sweet enough to rewatch the entire first season with me in prep for the second, and that's after having read the books, so it was truly selfless.

This is the courtly love of the modern era.

He tried to guide me through the labyrinthine plot, patiently explaining the characters' complex family trees and alliances, but I couldn't even keep their names straight. I made up my own nicknames and left him to interpret.

I'd say, "Oh, so Incest-Hottie killed the Dragon-Blonde's crazy dad?"

He'd translate: "Yes, Jaime Lannister killed Daenerys Targaryen's father, King Aerys Targaryen, a.k.a. the 'Mad King.' That's why they call Jaime 'Kingslayer.'"

Even the show bails on their real names.

It was after I caught up that the trouble started. Since my boyfriend works on Sunday nights, we promised to wait to watch each new episode until we could watch together.

But one night, he came over looking sheepish. "I have something to tell you . . ."

Never words a girl likes to hear. My mind raced through the terrible options: You cheated, you're getting back with your ex, you're moving abroad, you're ga—

". . . I watched *Game of Thrones* already."

BETRAYED!

I had to know the details. "When?"

"Three days ago."

Twist the knife, why don't you?

It wasn't so much that he watched it that made me mad—people slip up—but that he delayed telling me. It had taken all my willpower to resist watching the episode on my DVR. I thought our *Game of Thrones* relationship was exclusive.

"But I'll watch it again with you," he said.

So we tried that. But watching a show twice within days is boring, and bored men can think of only one thing. His mind and hands would wander, and I'd swat him away.

It's not you, it's HBO.

It was my turn to get him addicted to a show with *Breaking Bad*. I binge-watched the first four seasons on DVD and thought it was the best thing I'd ever seen. No junkie likes to be alone, so I got him hooked by rewatching the first season.

When his band had to go away on tour, I gave him the entire DVD set to catch up on the road. We planned to watch the fifth and final season together.

That was last December.

He had nine months to catch up, yet he only got halfway through season three. Women give birth in less time.

But he was busy living his life—priorities?—and we're both to blame, because we thoughtlessly spent our time together in other ways and neglected our TV homework. It didn't seem like an issue until the final season began airing this August.

And now I can't tell him anything.

It's torture! I never keep secrets from him—except for my real weight, my "number," my elaborate skin-care rituals, what I tweeze, or that I have ever in my life farted—but other than that, no secrets!

We share everything, our hopes, fears, dreams, colds, and yet I can't tell him what happened to Hank in the last episode. And did you *see* last week's episode?

Okay, sorry. No spoilers.

And I won't be able to hide my face in his shoulder when they do what you *know* they're going to do to Jesse before the series ends.

This is not a spoiler. It's an inevitability. Prepare yourselves.

But this, too, was unavoidable. My boyfriend is on tour again now, and he'll miss the series finale, so even if he had caught up, I'd have to go it alone.

Why don't I hold off watching the finale and wait for him?

I'm spoiled.

# Engagement Ring-A-Ding Ding

---

by Lisa

Valentine's Day is upon us, and if you're single, you know what that means.

Depression, shame, and chocolate cake.

I'm not saying you should feel that way. I'm just saying you might, if you're single, divorced, a widower, or a widow.

And if you do, I have a few words on the subject.

But before I begin, I have to admit that I've had more than a few Valentine's Days by myself, so much so that I've even written about it several times already.

Top that, for pathetic.

You can't.

But what I wrote before, and what I still believe, is that love is all around you. And you can't control whether you get love, but you can control whether you give it, and your heart won't know the difference.

If your heart were that smart, it would be your brain.

So this Valentine's Day, love something.

I'm going to be loving Daughter Francesca, Mother Mary, Brother Frank, besties Laura and Franca, and all my girlfriends, plus my furry and feathered family, including two puppies who right now are sharing my lap.

I'm not exactly proud to admit that I have a two-puppy lap.

But I took it one step further this year, and did something I never did before. I bought myself a present for Valentine's Day.

I know it's going to sound strange, but the present is a diamond ring.

Jewelers call it a right-hand ring, because the way the jewelry world sees it, the only way to get an engagement ring is if somebody else gives one to you.

And then you have to marry them.

I disagree, respectfully.

On both counts.

I've done all the marrying I'm going to do, and I've never regretted either divorce, not for a minute. I don't miss Thing One or Thing Two, but there is something I did miss.

The diamond.

And I've learned that if there's something you really want, the best course is to get it for yourself, instead of waiting for somebody else to give it to you.

So I bought myself an engagement ring.

You know why?

Because I'm still engaged.

Let me explain.

I think that the people I've mentioned above, the single, divorced, or widowed, sometimes feel left out of life in general, especially as we get older. I'm honest enough to admit that I've felt that way sometimes, and I definitely know girlfriends who do. It's easy to feel that way if you're not one of a couple, like you're a little bit of an odd duck, out of the mainstream.

Marginalized, or on the sidelines.

You find yourself going to movies with couples or sitting with them at weddings, which can be awkward and uncomfortable. Or it just gets old, as you get old.

And in time, you stop bothering.

You quit going to things, you opt out. You stay home. You make excuses.

Bottom line, you stop being engaged.

Allow me to suggest that that's not a great idea.

Life is meant to be lived, not viewed from the sidelines, and if you're not part of a team, there's nothing wrong with an individual sport.

So come out and play.

I still go alone to lots of things I get invited to, and now I have my pretty sparkly ring to remind me to live my life, and on my own terms.

And make myself happy.

You may not be as literal as I am, and you may not need a ring to remind you to stay engaged.

Or you might be a little more careful with your money.

But I'm wearing the prettiest engagement ring I ever owned, and I know I'm going to spend the rest of my life with the person who gave it to me.

For better or for worse.

In sickness and in health.

I do.

Happy Valentine's Day.

# Extremely Speedy Delivery

By Lisa

Do you remember when you wanted mail?

I don't.

If you do, you must be younger than I am, or have a better memory, which is basically the same thing.

Bottom line, I'm not sure when this happened, but there came a time when mail started to suck.

Correction. I know exactly when this happened.

When I grew up and started paying my own bills.

We can all agree that bills are no fun, but that's not even the problem I have with my mail. Because at least bills are important. After all, they mean I did something or used something or ate something or bought something, and now it's time to pay the piper.

This is America.

And I get that.

The problem is that the bills are the best part of my mail, which tells you how much my mail sucks.

I don't know why I bother walking to my mailbox every day, and to tell you the truth, I don't bother. I let the mail pile up, and the only reason I get it after a few days is that I want people to know I'm still alive.

My mailbox is at the end of the driveway, but it's barely worth the walk to get a flurry of coupons I can't use, Valpak's for mediocre Chinese restaurants, offers for free vacations that aren't really free, or cards with an 800 number I can call to claim unclaimed property or freight that I know will not belong to me.

I have all my property.

And I divorced all my freight.

Most of the time, I walk from my mailbox directly to the recycling bin. In fact, if the mail were addressed to my recycling bin, that would save a lot of time.

But yesterday I got the suckiest piece of mail ever, and I thought I would share with you, because I bet you don't live within a ten-mile radius of a nuclear reactor.

Like I do.

Did I mention I'm selling the house, as of today?

I didn't even know I lived within ten miles of a nuclear reactor until I got the notice in the mail.

Well, come to think of it, I knew there was something vaguely nuclear in the distance because I could see the weird towers, but I figured they were farther away than ten miles.

Like maybe in Detroit.

Also, now that you mention it, I hear an earsplitting alarm the first Monday of every month, which is testing the system for nuclear emergency, but who doesn't need a good alarm on a Monday?

Also the nuclear reactor is in a town called Limerick, and you can understand how this name contributed to my denial. Limerick reminds me of shamrocks, leprechauns, and green happiness in general.

Erin Go Boom!

If I were going to locate a nuclear reactor anywhere, I would name the town something as appealing as Limerick, too.

Like Luckyville.

Or Moneytown.

Or Lotsasinglemenburg.

And the company that runs the nuclear reactor is called Exelon, which is another great name.

My nuclear company would be called Awesomey.

Or Fantasticon!

Or Besty McBesterson Enterprises.

Anyway, to return to the mail, it was a cheery pastel-colored brochure, which I thought was for another lame Chinese restaurant until I opened it and read the top of the first page:

WHAT IS RADIATION?

Answer: you don't want to know.

But it's good you like green, because that's your new skin color in the event of a nuclear emergency.

I read through the pamphlet, which contained a section on how to prepare for the emergency, and it suggested that first thing, I should pack my portable radio.

I'll get right on that. I'm sure it's around somewhere, like in 1965.

The brochure also said that in the event of a nuclear accident, I should stock up on potassium iodide, but I'm pretty sure I have a couple of bananas lying around, which is probably the same thing.

Finally, the brochure made clear that in the event of an evacuation, only service animals will be permitted inside shelters.

No problem.

I'm getting maids outfits for all the dogs and cats.

They're serving me as we speak.

# Frankenfood

---

By Lisa

I have good news for you, and it concerns carbohydrates.

Somebody in New York came up with the cronut.

In case you haven't heard, a cronut is a cross between a croissant and a doughnut, and people are lining up around the block for them. In some bakeries, they cost $40, and scalpers are even selling them for $100.

Trust me, if a food has a scalper, it's either a carbohydrate or crack cocaine.

Cronuts are so popular that one newspaper called them a "viral dessert."

I'm not sure this would be my word choice.

I generally like to separate my desserts from my viruses.

I quarantine my food.

Cronuts come rolled in sugar, filled with cream, or topped with glaze, and bottom line, I can't wait to get my lips around one.

Maybe that came out wrong.

I might be on the next train to New York.

The bakery is in SoHo. I'm gonna be SoHappy.

People are saying that cronuts are the new cupcakes, but I

never believe it when people say something is the new something else.

Except that seventy is the new fifty.

Speaking as someone over fifty, I can tell you that's true.

But not if you eat a lot of cronuts.

Don't get cronutty.

If you ask me, the cronut is the high-rent version of Dunkin' Donuts' new Glazed Doughnut Breakfast Sandwich.

Yes, you read that right. Dunkin' Donuts has come up with the idea of putting eggs and bacon between slices of a glazed doughnut, and they're hoping you stick it in your mouth.

I will, except for the bacon.

I never eat anything smarter than I am.

Unless it's a carbohydrate.

I'm trying to understand when the combination platter turned into the combination food.

Because it's obviously brilliant.

Why eat your eggs and then a doughnut, when you can stick them together and shove them in your mouth?

Think of the time you're saving!

Plus it all goes down the same.

If it doesn't lodge in your throat and choke you to death.

You remember the Monster Mash.

It was a graveyard smash.

In fact, why not mash all your food up?

For example, we love mashed potatoes. So I bet we would love mashed potatoes carrots oatmeal pizza.

It would completely do away with side orders, but who cares?

They're so . . . side.

And it doesn't matter if one of these things is not like the other.

Don't be so matchy-matchy about your food.

Think outside the box bag carton tube toilet paper.

The culinary times are changing, and we have to change with them.

After all, we live in the era of mash-ups. I heard this term so much that I went online to see what it meant, and found the definition in the urban dictionary.

By the way, don't ask me why it's called "urban."

Maybe to use it, you have to live in the city.

I'm guessing New York City.

Probably SoHo.

No. No.

Anyway the urban dictionary defines mash-up as "to take two completely different types of music and put them together."

Great idea, right?

Just think how awesome it would be if Jay-Z and Bjorn were in the same song.

Agree?

Sorry, I can't hear you. The music is too loud. Or maybe there's a head-on collision between two freight trains.

In my head.

You could even mash-up your clothes. After all, we know how great it looks when you wear stripes with polka dots.

Like a rodeo clown!

When I was little, if something was mashed-up, it meant it was broken. You could look up the word in the Dictionary, which was an antique thing called a Book, found someplace called a Bookstore or a Library.

Photographs of these things are available online, and I encourage you to know your nation's history.

But nowadays we're mashing up our food.

I say it's time to throw away our plates.

And get a trough.

# Demanding

---

By Lisa

It was the great philosopher Justin Bieber who said, "Never say never," and boy, that kid knew what he was talking about.

Because lately I find myself doing things I never thought I'd do.

Things I'd read about other people doing and thought to myself, I may do a lot of things, but I'll never do *that*.

It started three weeks ago, when I was looking for something to watch on TV and nothing was on, so I defaulted to On Demand. I'm a big fan of On Demand, mostly because I'm not the demanding type and it's training me to assert myself.

After all, how often do you get to say, "This is what I want, and I want it right now."

Right.

Or if you get to say it, how often does anybody do it?

Same here.

So I've become On Demanding.

I finally found somebody to do exactly what I want, the very moment that I want it, and his name is Sony.

I wish I could marry him and make him Mr. Scottoline.

Sony Scottoline.

You know what we would name our son?

Tony.

Tony Sony Scottoline.

I started scrolling around the On Demand menu for TV series and figured I'd give *Dexter* a shot, since I'd never seen it. I watched the first episode and liked it, so I figured I'd watch the second, and before you can say "blood spatter," I had watched seven years of *Dexter*.

That would be twelve episodes a year, and the show has run for seven seasons, so I watched 7 × 12 episodes, and each episode is about an hour.

I'll leave the math to you. Because I did the calculation and I already know the answer:

It's way too much television.

Not only that, but I watched all seven years in a matter of days, which means almost continuously. I had it on in my office while I worked, and I watched it during lunch and dinner. It kept me up past my bedtime, and I even got up early one morning before breakfast, to squeeze in another ep.

Yes, I say ep.

That's how I talk now.

Because I'm too busy watching television to take the time to say episode.

I had read about people who binge-watch television and thought, I'll never do that, but who was I kidding?

I binge-read, I binge-work, and I binge-eat. In fact, I might be a binge-binger.

And once I started watching *Dexter,* I knew that I was going to finish all of it, but not in a good way, like when you start college and know you're going to graduate. It was more in a chocolate-cake way, in that I know if there is chocolate cake in the house, I'm going to eat it all gone.

So I ate *Dexter* all gone.

Or put differently, I got a Ph.D. in *Dexter.*

There's another thing I'm doing that I never thought I'd do, and I'm thinking it might be related, but you be the judge.

Just don't judge too harshly.

We all know that I sleep with three dogs, namely, Ruby, Peach, and Tony. And I have the two puppies, Kit and Boone, who are about seven months old and sleep in my bedroom, but they sleep together in their cage.

Let me hasten to point out that the puppies love their cage. At bedtime, they run into it happily, cuddle up together, and fall asleep.

But one night, I looked over at the puppies in their cage, and they looked back at me, in my nice comfy bed, with the other three dogs.

So you know where this is going.

I never thought I would sleep with five dogs.

But now we sleep together, all five of us in the nice comfy bed.

And tonight, we're starting *Game of Thrones*.

# Old MacDonald Takes Manhattan

By Francesca

City dwellers can be a little snobby. Okay, a lot snobby. And I admit to buying into the idea that New York City has the best of everything—the best museums, the best theater, the best music, and the best restaurants. I thought the mere fact of living here elevated my taste.

But not when it comes to food.

I hate to burst the city bubble, but fancy restaurants don't cut it. To really educate my palate, I had to talk to some farmers.

Every Saturday, a farmers' market pops up in a small park near my apartment. The transformation alone is impressive. On weekdays, it's just a normal park full of benches and plants that endure more animal/drunk person urine than God intended, but come Saturday—BOOM—it's an Eden of organic produce and wholesome, shiny-faced people who are cheerful at seven in the morning, and probably earlier, at whatever time they have to leave their magical farms far far away from the city.

I first started going to the farmers' market because it's the only place I can go food shopping with a dog. I have a vague understanding that GMOs are bad, but I feel most strongly about making dull errands into fun outings with my dog.

If there were a licensed dentist that did business in the street, I'd give it a shot just to have Pip on my lap.

So I leashed up the dog, put on my cutest pretend-I'm-going-to-the-gym outfit, and headed to market.

Right off the bat I got the idea that I'm doing it wrong, because while I was looking to buy all the conventional foods: chicken eggs, romaine lettuce, Jersey tomatoes, the people around me are getting duck eggs, "dinosaur" kale, and small, discolored "heirloom" tomatoes.

I had much to learn.

After the age of six, it's embarrassing not to know the names of fruits and vegetables. But I was completely stumped by a pile of mystery veggies that looked like bright green *churros,* minus the cinnamon and sugar. I swallowed my pride and asked the female farmer what they were.

"Okra."

I thought that was a color.

"Most people describe it as slimy," she added.

Now there's a winning advertising campaign.

I passed on the slimy *churros* but chuckled at a sign that read "Young Lettuce."

"Oh, we're lucky we got that this week," she said. "Young lettuce is more tender and silky. It's so delicate, it practically melts in your mouth."

I was *this close* to calling Produce Protective Services.

I backed away from the pedo-farmer and bought a bunch of barely legal arugula instead.

Next, I went to a poultry and dairy farm stand to buy eggs and yogurt, and as I was paying, a woman pushing a baby stroller came up beside me. I didn't hear what product she asked for at first, but she had a complaint about last week's purchase that pricked my ears.

"There were black spots last time," I heard her say.

*Oh no,* I thought, *might the eggs be bad?*

"That can be the result of natural bruising or marks from the yard," said the farmer. "They are free-range, after all."

The woman nodded. "All right, I'll take another bag."

*Bag?*

The farmer reached into his cooler and pulled out a plastic bag of severed chicken feet.

And I thought I was adventurous for getting *Greek* yogurt.

The only meat I eat is fish, but the line at the fishmonger is always superlong. At first, I thought it must be because the seafood is so fresh and delicious. Then I noticed the line consisted of mostly women. Then I noticed these women, young and old, were buying a hell of a lotta fish.

Then I noticed the fisherman.

When I say "fisherman," you might think Gorton's. Instead, think Romance Novel. Think Daniel Day Lewis in *Last of the Mohicans,* but in an Irish knit. Long, dark hair roughly tied back, skin only so weathered as to connote experience, not age, eyes squinting slightly, not from the sun, but from looking into your soul.

If mermaids were real, he'd have no trouble catching them.

I don't have the money to buy extra filets just to talk to him, so instead I stall by asking him for cooking tips.

"Uh, a squeeze of lemon, maybe a little olive oil," he says.

"Should I bake it, or pan-cook it?" I bat my lashes.

He shrugs. "Either, I guess."

Stop it, you're making me blush.

Okay, so maybe fisher-hottie isn't biting. But I have learned to cook a great tuna steak, fried flounder fish tacos, sole meunière, and the perfect seared scallop.

On the other hand, my dog, Pip, gets everyone to fall in love with him. He gets a treat at every stand, and sometimes two.

At this point, Pip thinks the farmers raise antibiotic-free Milk-Bones and organic Beggin' Strips.

With each Saturday I spent hanging out at the farmers' market, I grew a little more sophisticated. Now I pay extra for raw honey with bits of honeycomb and "bee debris" in it, because the heat treatment of conventional honey kills its natural vitamins and nutrients. I make blistered shishito peppers as an afternoon snack. And I speak fluent kale: I can tell the difference between curly, rainbow, and Russian kale, but I also know that Tuscan, Lacinato, and dinosaur kale are all the same thing.

Maybe one day, I'll even try the okra.

# Desitin Days

---

By Lisa

I came back from book tour with something for Mother's Day.

Diaper rash.

Yes, you read that correctly.

I'd been on a book tour that started in Philadelphia and traveled all over the country in the same jeans. I had no way to wash them, and I only have one pair.

That I can fit into.

I wore the jeans on the planes, in the hotel rooms, during the signings, out to dinner with readers and booksellers—anyway, you get the idea. What happened was that I started to chafe in Buckhead, which is too ritzy an Atlanta suburb to start itching in your pants.

Call it The Sisterhood of the Traveling Itchy Pants.

So I went to see what was going on down there. It's not a region I usually visit, as I have better things to do. In fact, the last time I inspected myself was when I was thirteen and trying to learn how to use a tampon, folded directions in hand.

Too much information? Welcome to our book. Every woman in the world knows exactly what I'm talking about. Men, I trust your intelligence to follow along.

It wasn't easy to inspect myself, given the location of the problem, and I didn't have a hand mirror. The only mirror available in the hotel was over the bathroom sink, and to put it in a ladylike fashion, my hips don't move that way.

Anymore.

The only way to see the rash was to take my iPhone, switch it to the camera function, then put it on the selfie setting, as if I were taking my own picture.

Or sexting myself.

Anyway, and I'll say this as gently as possible, what I saw in my iPhone was that the chafing had morphed into a pink rash on my inner thighs. At first I thought it was athlete's foot, just higher up, but there's no such thing. Then I thought it was bedbugs, but thanks to my wonderful publisher, I was staying at the Ritz.

So I did what I always do with any kind of problem.

I denied it.

Rashes and problems do not go away if they're ignored, and by San Francisco, I was whipping out my iPhone in every ladies' room and watching the spread of my rash, which was forming a relief map of the seven continents. It went from a pretty pink to an ugly red, although at least it hid my cellulite.

I took pictures, and in no circumstances will I show them to you.

By Los Angeles, not only was it itching, but hurting. By Houston, I started walking like a cowboy and fit right in.

By then I got on the Internet, found pictures of my condition, and diagnosed myself. At age fifty-seven, I had given myself diaper rash. So I took myself to CVS, where I bought the remedy recommended, namely, a tube that read BOUDREAUX'S BUTT PASTE.

I'm not making this name up, and I can imagine your incredulous reaction, because I saw it on the face of the TSA agent who took it out of my Ziploc bag at airport security. He stared in disbelief at the tube, probably trying to decide if it was a joke, then said: "Miss, this exceeds four ounces. You can't take it on board."

My embarrassment turned to desperation. "Sir, I'm begging you. This is a medication, and I need it desperately. If you don't believe me, I can show you a picture that will make you throw up."

The TSA agent met my gaze, returned the tube of butt paste to the bag, and handed it to me. "Okay, take it. I understand, I got kids."

So for once, I got the government off my butt.

Of course, I thought this was funny enough to call Mother Mary and tell her, especially since it was almost Mother's Day. "Ma," I said. "Guess what? I couldn't wash my jeans and now I have diaper rash."

"You're a dirty pig."

But I know she meant it, with love.

Happy Mother's Day!

# Mother Mary Talks to God and Luis

By Lisa

I visited Mother Mary, but it wasn't all laughs.

I had a night free on book tour in Naples, Florida, so I made the trip to Miami to take her out to dinner for Mother's Day. I arrived to pick her up, but she wasn't dressed, because she had decided she didn't want to go.

"We should stay home and order Papa John's," she said, frowning.

"Ma, you can't have Papa John's on Mother's Day."

"Why not?"

"Let me take you out."

"No."

"Please. It's my Mother's Day, too."

"Hmph." So Mother Mary went into her bedroom to change her clothes. She emerged in a nice black top and long skirt, but something was missing.

"Ma, you're not wearing a bra?"

"Why should I?"

I paused. "I'll give you two reasons. Right and left."

"No. No more bras."

"Ma, you have to."

"No I don't. I'm eighty-nine."

"Yes, you do. You're eighty-nine."

"No."

"Yes." We reach an impasse, which she breaks.

"I'll wear something over the top. It's the same thing."

"Okay, good idea," I say, relieved. Any women over fifty knows camouflage trumps support.

But Mother Mary comes out of her bedroom in her lab coat. She's only four-foot-eleven, so it reaches to her ankles, and with her snowy white hair, she looks like a superannuated Doogie Howser.

"Ma. No lab coat. It's too nice a restaurant."

"So what?"

"Please, Doc. You're not on call tonight."

"I need the pockets."

"You have a purse." I form praying hands. "I'm begging you."

Mother Mary rolls her eyes. "Fine."

I hurry into her bedroom, grab an embroidered jacket I got her from Chico's, and dress her as if she were a stubborn child. "There."

"*Now* will you shut up?"

I can't, yet. "What about your hearing aids?"

"No."

"Ma, please wear them. I'll have to shout at you."

"No, you won't. I'm fine."

"Okay," I say, after a moment. I won on the pizza, and I know when to fold 'em, but I want to cheer her up. I reach for my phone. "Let me take a picture of you. You look so cute."

She rolls her eyes again. "Come on. Always with that stupid camera."

"Please, we can send it to Francesca."

"Fine."

Later at the restaurant, I'm about to ask for a quiet table when I see that the place is completely empty because we've arrived at six o'clock, which is too early for dinner in South Beach. We sit down, I order a margarita, and Mother Mary orders a Bud Lite, but they only have Amstel Light, so she sniffs. "Fine."

She's saying fine so often that I know nothing is fine. "Ma, are you okay?"

"I had a talk with God about when I was going to die."

*Bam.* "Okay." I try not to look surprised, and I shouldn't be. The Flying Scottolines have a history of bringing up personal subjects in public. For example, Mother Mary told me she wanted a mausoleum while we were in the produce aisle at Whole Foods. My brother told me he was gay when we were standing on a city street. I told you in print that I have diaper rash.

See what I mean?

We lack boundaries. The Western Hemisphere is our living room.

Mother Mary frowns. "God told me I have to live until I'm 110."

My chest feels tight, and I wish my margarita would come. "Okay, so that's good news, right?"

At this point a different waiter comes over, and he's tall, young, and handsome. Like everybody in this town, he looks like a model. He sets a beer in front of my mother, flashing her a dazzling smile. "Why, you look lovely tonight, young lady."

"Thank you." Mother Mary brightens. "What's your name?"

"Luis."

"I'm Mary. This is my daughter. She has a camera. She's crazy with that camera." She gestures at me. "Get your camera, honey. Take a picture of me and Luis."

Luis snuggles my mother while I grab my phone and take a picture. They both look adorable.

Mother Mary smiles up at Luis. "Thanks, doll."

"No problem, Mary," he answers, then leaves.

Mother Mary looks flushed. "He has bedroom eyes," she says, then laughs.

I laugh with her. "Hubba hubba."

"So I was telling you about God. He said, 110. Maybe 112, tops."

"And that's fine with you, right?"

Mother Mary grins. "Absolutely fine."

# With Our Powers Combined

---

By Francesca

Some people have a freezer full of ice cream, frozen meats and veggies, maybe some leftovers. My freezer is full of trash.

I'm composting.

Compost is a fancy word for trash. Compost means only biodegradable food waste. Composting helps the environment.

Just not the environment of my apartment.

Food trash stinks, so during the week, I keep it all in a plastic bag in my freezer until Saturday, when I walk it to my local farmers' market where they have special receptacles for it, and there's a woman who acts as the Mistress of Compost. She's a fit, attractive Asian woman who keeps her hair buzzed short. Her typical uniform is cargo pants, boots, a white tee with rolled sleeves, and mirrored Aviator sunglasses. Oh, and dishwashing gloves.

She's like the GI Jane for the environmentally conscious.

I'm telling you, she's pretty fierce, and not just for a woman who hangs out by a Dumpster. Because her hands are inevitably covered in trash, she greets you by bumping elbows. Call it the Compost High Five.

My dog adores her. Finally, a woman who shares his love for

stinky trash. If she had used tissues falling out of her pocket, he might actually leave me for her.

And I like her, too. She has a passion for the environment, and she uses her considerable charisma to get people to listen to her from her trash-can pulpit. She convinced me that composting would be a cinch, and now I'd feel guilty to pass her on a Saturday without my bag of frozen trash.

With recycling, fear and guilt serve a higher purpose.

It's not just guilt; the psychology behind composting is complex. For me, it appeals to my dual inclinations to laziness and self-congratulation. I get to take the trash out less often during the week and feel like Captain Planet come Saturday.

That said, there are hazards. Everyday foods, when frozen, become an arsenal of tiny weaponry. Rotten asparagus forms daggers, poking holes through the plastic compost bag, so that when I pull it out of the freezer, it rains a trail of frozen vegetables. One time I spilled a bag of frozen kale, which crumbled like confetti all over my kitchen floor.

Unlike confetti, the pieces became instantly soggy and defied any attempt to vacuum them up. I had to sit on the floor and peel each one like scabs.

And then there's explaining it to people. I had friends over to watch the finale of the greatest TV show of all time, *Breaking Bad*. When my friend went to get ice cubes for our meth blue margaritas, she said, "Whoa, what's all this stuff in your freezer?"

"Oh, um, that's just my compost bags. The ice trays are probably behind it."

"What's all this black stuff?"

"Oh, that's just coffee grounds that spilled. Don't worry about it."

The downside of composting in an apartment is that there's

not much room in which to put it. I already have separate piles for newspapers, broken-down cardboard boxes, and bags for glass, plastic, and cans. I don't even have room for a normal waste bin; the bag for regular trash hangs from a clothes hanger in a coat closet.

But the upside of composting in an apartment is also that there's not much room. While the freezer offers the occasional inconvenience and embarrassment, my lack of space is my excuse for not going to the next level of home compost:

Worms.

That's right, a bin with live worms to eat through your bio-degradable waste and create fertilizer. Now, I don't want to deter anyone from doing this; I looked into it, and it sounds like a totally cool science experiment—if you have a backyard. I'm less open-minded when the worms are sharing my five hundred square feet of personal space.

Please, I finally got rid of my roommate.

So storing trash in my freezer each week is the least I can do, literally.

The truth is, I enjoy composting. I like the whole process, of taking a minute to be more conscious of the waste I'm putting out, walking to the farmers' market with it, and talking to the Compost Queen and the other people dropping off their trash. People who compost have a little extra compassion and kind-ness, and they're not afraid to get their hands dirty. It's a nice community to be a part of, the composters.

And it's good to be reminded of that other nice community I'm lucky to be a part of:

Earth.

# God, Man, and Prada

---

By Lisa

You may have heard that the Pope is stepping down because he no longer feels he can do the job.

Congress should take a lesson.

Consider that the Pope got his job from God, and he just quit.

Congress got their jobs from mere human beings, yet they would never dream of quitting, despite the fact that they cannot perform the most basic function of government, like making a budget.

They don't have the decency to step down.

Or the grace.

Like His Grace.

As if between the Pope and Congress, only one of these is supposed to admit that he is fallible.

And the wrong one just admitted it.

I'm trying to imagine the enormity of the ego that allows you to think you're entitled to your job, which has great pay and benefits, even though you don't do it. You must think you're handpicked by God, or at least a flock of cardinals.

But no.

The guy who was handpicked by God and the cardinals is the one who just packed up his desk.

The guys who failed to do their jobs just took a vacation. With pay. And benefits.

Because Congress's pay and benefits are always included in the budget.

That is job one in Washington, and it's the only job that gets done.

I give the Pope a lot of credit for stepping down, considering the great privileges that come with his position. He did the unselfish thing for the greater good. Also he had to give up a gorgeous pair of red shoes, made by Prada.

Now we're talking sacrifice.

By the way, the Pope is the only one on the planet allowed to wear those red shoes, which guarantees that he'll never find himself on the losing end of a who-wore-it-better picture.

Don't you hate it when you go to a party and someone walks in wearing the same vestments?

Congress seems unfamiliar with the concept of the greater good. This is unfortunate, given that they are in the greater-good business, but there's only so much you can ask of the American worker.

Correction.

Congress is made up of the people who allegedly work for the American worker, but they're on vacation now, which they call recess.

Because they act like third-graders.

Congress doesn't make clear how many recesses it takes a year. I know because I tried to figure it out online, and I'm sure this is completely inadvertent, or maybe for the greater good.

I did find a congressional recess schedule, but it was completely impossible to read. However, if you have so many recesses that you need a schedule for them, you have too many recesses.

I did read online that some members of Congress want to rename their recesses and call them "district work periods."

I think this is a great idea. I'm thinking of renaming my cellulite and calling it "muscle."

Congress has a lot of unusual names for things. For example, they call their inability to reach a budget *the sequester*.

This is a hard term to understand, because it comes from the Latin word *sequestrare,* which means *to remove* or *separate*. Allow me to use the word in a sentence for you, so you can understand it:

Congress is sequestered from reality.

See?

It's interesting that in a time when the Catholic Church has decided to abandon the Latin Mass, Congress has decided to become a Classics major.

I took four years of Latin, but I will never understand Congress.

Because I speak English.

By the way, Congress itself comes from the Latin word *congressus,* which means *meeting* or *intercourse*.

I will leave to you which meaning is more relevant to Congress.

And I will remind you that Congress is on vacation, so it isn't meeting.

My guess is that it's having vacation intercourse, which we all know is the best kind.

Except that they're not the ones getting screwed.

# Hobby Horse

---

By Lisa

I'm trying to decide if I should start a garden.

Or if I do, will I turn it into meth for the menopausal?

These are the kind of questions that occur to me when I have a few days off, between books. I'm supposed to sit on my duff, but I do that for a living, so when I have nothing to do, I tend to get very active.

Last time I painted my downstairs.

Enough said.

This would be part of my tendency to overdo everything. In my view, whoever said "less is more" is wrong. Life is an *all-you-can-eat* buffet, and less isn't enough.

Less isn't even a good start.

Because of this, I've learned I have to be careful with hobbies. Give me even the smallest pleasure, and I can turn it into work, complete with a Things To Overdo List that never gets completely (over)done, which leads to a generalized feeling of guilt.

Guilt is not the purpose of a hobby.

So I hear.

Anyway, I sort of backed into the gardening idea. It started because I was thinking about fencing in my backyard, because I'd like the ability to let the dogs out sometimes, without walking them. I have five dogs and I walk them five times a day, and you can do the math.

Bottom line, it's a lot of dog walking.

See what I mean, about overdoing things?

To stay on track, the truth is, I don't really mind walking the dogs, even when people stop me, and say, "Got your hands full!" and "Who's walking who?" and "Are they all yours?"

To this last question, most times I answer yes, but sometimes I say, "No, I'm just the dog walker. I would never have five dogs. Whoever has five dogs must be crazy. Or menopausal."

Sometimes I even plead the fifth. (Dog.)

Anyway, so I was thinking if I fenced in my backyard, I could let the dogs out to play and run around, which would be fun for them. But that got me wondering about what kind of fence to get, and since I'm not a big fan of fences, somebody suggested that I get a wire-mesh fence and plant knockout roses on either side of it, so you couldn't even see the fence.

I never heard of knockout roses, but the idea knocked me out.

So I went online and started looking at photos of knockout roses, then photos of other flowers and gardens, and before you know it, I got the idea of putting in a "cottage" garden.

You don't need a cottage to have a "cottage" garden.

You could just have a "house."

Wikipedia gave me the idea that a "cottage" garden is a fancy way of saying an "informal" garden, which I translated as a fancy way of saying, "garden for lazy people."

Me!

So I started looking for books about cottage gardens, and it took me an hour to choose three, since there are 29,474 books on the subject. The books come in, I sit down to study, and in five pages, I realize that a cottage garden isn't for lazy people.

In fact, I learn that the only garden for lazy people is no garden.

And I have that already.

But that only makes me want to garden more, because I'm starting to smell New Hobby That I Can Turn Into Guilt.

So I hit the books, take notes, and draw up planting charts. I learn that a cottage garden should have roses, and there are 203,934,847 types of roses to choose from, though only 39,734,727 do well in my planting zone, which narrows it down.

By the way, my planting zone is 6.

It's my chance to be a six!

I try to decide between bourbon roses, noisette roses, provence roses, and you get the idea, then turn to climbing plants, where I have to choose between European or Japanese honeysuckle.

What, no Italian-American honeysuckle?

Then I move on to hedging plants like viburnum and clematis.

Don't ask me what these words mean.

I never heard them before either.

But they sound dirty, like every girl should have a viburnum for her clematis.

Ahem.

Also a cottage garden is supposed to have herbs like southernwood, wormwood, catmint, feverfew, lungwort, soapwort, hyssop, and sweet woodruff.

In other words, Harry Potter, in pots.

I get dizzy from the words and colors and the chance to use four years of Latin.

I *knew* it would come in handy!

The more I read, the more excited I get about my soon-to-be cottage garden.

The five dogs watch me, wondering if it comes with a fence.

Of course it does.

But only if they do the pruning.

# King Baby

---

By Lisa

I wished I lived in New York, so I could vote for Anthony Weiner and Eliot Spitzer.

I want them around for a long, long time.

Very long.

Not that size matters.

Theirs, anyway.

I don't care what they're running for, just so they win. I want them in the TV news all the time. I need something good to watch, now that the royal baby is all grown-up.

In fact, I think that we need more wieners in Washington. I bet the country would run a lot better if our politicians spent less time in Congress and more time in the bathroom taking pictures of themselves in their underwear.

Got junk?

Consider Anthony Weiner, who was kicked out of Congress for showing his wiener, then he gave interviews to *People* magazine and the *New York Times* saying he was a changed wiener.

Not exactly.

Because even as he was giving the interview, he was sending pictures of his wiener to young girls and calling himself Carlos Danger.

There is so much to admire in this, I don't know where to begin.

I make up names for a living, and I could never have thought of a name as cool as Carlos Danger. You have to have the imagination of a six-year-old to come up with something like that, and isn't childlike innocence something we all admire in our elected leaders?

He should win a magic decoder ring!

He could give it to the NSA.

Second, I think too many wieners give up too easy, but not this wiener. Even after he gets fired, it doesn't stop him, and that's the kind of persistence that pays off. It's just like the movie *Rudy,* except that it's just plain *Rude.*

Or *Randy.*

To be fair, sometimes Congress does show atypical persistence. For example, it failed to shut down the government over the budget last time, so it's going to try again.

Yay!

They're just not trying hard enough.

Try harder, wieners!

Also, Anthony Weiner is excellent at fooling people, like *People* magazine and the *New York Times.*

You have to hand it to the guy.

Well, not that hand.

The other one.

Honestly, do you think you could fool *People* magazine or the *New York Times* about anything?

I couldn't.

Well, maybe *People* magazine.

At least I can do their crossword puzzle.

But not the *New York Times.*

I couldn't fool the *New York Times* about anything.

Have you seen me on Halloween? Even when I was little, I couldn't convince my neighbors that I was a princess or a hobo.

And last year, they all knew it was me.

I should have gone as a wiener.

And to succeed in government, you have to be able to fool people. In fact, to succeed in government, you have to be a world-class fooler of people.

I think both wieners have proven themselves, don't you?

They fooled everybody, not only magazines and newspapers, but you, me, their wives, their dogs, and their babies.

I bet they could even fool the royal baby.

I admire Eliot Spitzer for all of the same reasons, and then some. You might remember that he was fired because he went to prostitutes, but to me, I think that qualifies him as a great politician.

He's a job creator, people.

With unemployment at an all-time high, Eliot Spitzer was just doing his part.

Well, not *that* part.

This part.

And he fooled people, at the same time. Isn't that the type of multitasking we need in our leaders?

I bet Eliot Spitzer could hire a prostitute, take a picture of himself in his underwear, and fool people, all at the same time.

So I say, vote for Anthony Weiner and Eliot Spitzer!

They're our royal babies.

# Politics and Farm-Fresh Eggs

## By Francesca

Today I voted for the first time in New York.

I had been reluctant to relinquish my Pennsylvania swing-state-voter status; three things made me register to vote in New York City: Eliot Spitzer, Anthony Weiner, and my local farmers' market.

I had never felt more alienated from my adopted city than when I heard people defending Eliot Spitzer and Anthony Weiner. With regard to Spitzer, any man who believes he is entitled to purchase a woman's body for sex cannot possibly respect a woman as an equal. Only objects can be bought, and objects are not equal to humans. I want a representative who is real clear on which one of these I am.

As for Weiner, all of his sexting partners, consensual and non-consensual, began as female political supporters who reached out to him on the topic of politics. This was not Rielle Hunter going up to John Edwards saying, "You are so hot." These women reached out to Weiner on the topic of politics, and, after occasionally humoring them, he consistently transitioned the conversation to sex. If I ask my mayor a question or raise an issue at a town-hall meeting, I want to believe he's actually listening to me, not imagining what I look like naked.

So, my stubborn desire to be viewed as a human being instead of a blow-up doll got me interested in New York politics. What got me to register to vote were volunteers.

Every Saturday morning, I go to the local farmers' market, and this summer I started noticing a lot of unusually friendly folks mixed in with the power-grannies sniffing the melons and the yoga-dolls buying kale. Who were these smiling strangers?

Politicians.

And their dutiful, overworked volunteers.

If you don't know one personally, it's easy to dismiss political volunteers as a nuisance, but I think they're pretty cool. They care about something enough to stand outside and talk to you about it, so already I like them more than many of my peers.

And when you talk to politicians, you'll likely get a rehearsed statement in defensively vague language, their real opinions hidden behind a wall of glossy white teeth. But a political volunteer will answer your questions like a human being.

Because he or she still is one.

When I talked to the volunteers, they didn't blink if I stopped them mid spiel and asked something like, "So what's wrong with the other guy?"

This is where the good dirt is. I heard all kinds of juicy stories.

Because politics is just gossip on steroids, and the girls' bathroom is D.C.

Lately, the men's locker room is Manhattan.

In the course of my farmers' market debates, I also came to believe that we should all try to be extra nice to political volunteers when we encounter them, because so many others are downright abusive.

I watched an older gentleman go from quietly purchasing pasture-raised, cruelty-free chicken eggs to shouting in the face of a female volunteer, completely unprompted.

I get that we're all rage-aholics when it comes to discussing politics on TV or online, but let's bring a little humanity to our face-to-face interactions, hmm? Be at least as humane as we are to the chickens.

So I learned an awful lot about my city and the candidates trying to improve it, and I met some friendly, intelligent people in my dealings with the volunteers.

Plus, they gave treats to my dog.

So I registered to vote in the nick of time. That turned out to be the easy part.

In the past, when I voted in Pennsylvania, I went to my polling location at the nearby elementary school, like all of my neighbors within ten minutes' driving distance. There, I generally found the same group of people volunteering, and knew most by name. I don't remember ever waiting in a line.

This is what suburban democracy looks like.

In the city, after chatting a bit with the volunteer who gave me the registration forms, we discovered that we lived on the same street, one block away from each other.

"So where is our polling station?" I asked her.

"You have to look online. It depends on where you live."

"But . . . don't we live in the same place?"

Not same enough. She encouraged me to double-check, and when I did, I found that even though I pass her house every day on my dog walk, she and I do not go to the same polling location.

Ironically, mine was still an elementary school. Although this one had legions of volunteers, a line down the block of voters, and, my favorite: signs outside saying "Vote Here" in English, Spanish, Chinese, Korean, and, I think, Hindi.

This is what urban democracy looks like.

And although I don't think the Founding Fathers could have ever imagined it, it's exactly what they meant.

Once inside, I actually felt nervous. The place was crowded, and I didn't want to be the person who held anyone up. I caught a glimpse behind the curtain as someone exited a booth and saw the voting machines were the old crank kind I had only heard of.

For all of New York City's modernity, you'd think they'd upgrade their voting machines from the butter-churning era.

Okay, so they might not be *that* old. But I'm just an impatient millennial; if it doesn't have a touch screen, I don't know how to use it.

Voting—is there an App for that?

So I stood in line, eavesdropping on the people ahead of me as they inquired about the voting directions, a last-minute cram session.

My tension eased when I saw the volunteer at my booth, an older woman with the eyes and smile of someone much younger.

"The first time I ever voted in New York City, the woman in front of me had voted in the very first election that allowed women the vote," she said. "We forget, but it really wasn't that long ago."

"It's my first time voting in New York today," I said quietly.

"It is?" the volunteer cried, her voice booming. "Good for you!"

When it was my turn, she helped show me how the machine worked without my having to ask, and I thanked her for her time. I made my choices, most well-informed decisions, admittedly a few "Woman or Italian" last-minute calls on the more obscure offices, and I pulled the crank to seal the deal with a satisfying *ka-chunk.*

Maybe there's merit to the old machines yet.

I popped out from the curtain feeling happy, an emotion rarely associated with politics. I was no longer angrily voting only to block the idiot frat boys from office. Instead, I was looking out for my neighbors and my home, like they were looking out for me. I felt more connected to the strangers around me, even—and especially—those who spoke languages I couldn't recognize on a sign, and I had a greater sense of ownership and belonging in my adopted city.

As I left, a man still in line delivered the ultimate New Yorker's reason to vote: "If you don't vote, you can't complain. And I love to bitch!"

# Handygirl

---

By Lisa

I just put in a hundred perennials, which if you're not famil-
iar with gardening terms, means that I never have to do this
again for the rest of my life.

Because perennials are supposed to be automatic, in that
they come back every summer.

Like a yeast infection.

It took me five days to plant a garden, because I made every
rookie mistake possible.

First, let me just say that I had no idea that gardening is so
much hard physical labor. I toted sod, plants, and big rocks, in
ninety-degree heat.

Gardening isn't a hobby, it's a chain gang.

My back, legs, and shoulders ache, my leg is swollen from a
sting, and I got scratches from rosebushes I bought when I was
temporarily insane.

There can be no other explanation for buying a plant that
bites.

The problem with gardening is that the very term is a eu-
phemism.

It fools you into thinking that you'll be swanning around a
bunch of flowers.

Wrong.

Remember when you delivered a baby? It was called labor for a reason, so you had fair warning. Because it's work. There's pushing and pulling and yanking and profanity.

And that's just conception.

Sorry.

Anyway, back to my mistakes. Second mistake, I bought plants online because they were cheaper, then I found out that the nursery near me is going out of business and everything there was 40 percent off.

What I had already spent.

The online plants didn't come when they were supposed to, so I started thinking I'd need more plants anyway, and I could get them cheap at the nursery. I read through my new perennials books, went to the nursery with my To Buy list, and they had none of them.

So I bought whatever perennials they had on sale.

It's the Going Out of Business Garden.

And for what these plants cost, it's going to put me out of business.

Anyway, the books said I had to take the grass off and make a bed.

I had no idea. I thought you could just plant flowers in grass. I should have known I'd screw up. I never make my bed.

Third mistake, I thought the garden was a big area, but I'm not good at eyeballing it, as my father always said. Of course I know there are tape measures, but how would you know how many plumbago plants you need to fill a foot of garden? Until yesterday I thought plumbago was a back problem.

Now plumbago is giving me a back problem.

Bottom line, it's a big garden, so I got a great handyman, Dale, to help me, which is what you do when you're divorced.

You hire a husband.

Anyway the first thing Dale said was, "there's a machine that takes off sod."

Oh.

So we found out the machine was called a sod cutter, and we rented one right away and started cutting the sod, which is the garden equivalent of scalping your grass.

It took all day, cutting and hauling the sod, then raking the bed so no grass seeds were left. Then we started putting in plants, with Dale doing the manly work of digging and me doing the girly work of putting in the potting soil and covering the hole.

I was a cover girl.

Yay!

Next mistake, we used up all the plants I had bought on sale, and still had two-thirds of the garden left. The online plants

**Hard labor but worth it.**

still weren't here, so I went back to the garden center and bought more plants.

Three times.

I no longer consulted the books.

I bought any perennial that wasn't nailed down.

I would have planted a file cabinet if they'd let me.

But now I'm finished, and it looks beautiful, and it was worth all the trouble, like a brand-new baby.

Who remembers their labor anyway?

Okay, I do.

# Mother Nature Is a Bad Mom

---

By Lisa

I started gardening to get closer to Mother Nature, but now I hate her.

Perhaps hate is too strong a word.

Let's just say that we're frenemies.

Because it turns out that Mother Nature is the ultimate mean girl.

Let me explain.

A few weeks ago, I planted and mulched a large perennial garden, which took five days of hard labor and was worth every minute. I had no idea how much I would love this garden, which was lush, fragrant, and colorful, blooming with purple hyssop, blue plumbago, pink roses, yellow and pink coneflower, black-eyed Susans, lavender, and daises.

You get the idea. It's pretty.

I watered it with sprinklers, probably too often, and I took tons of photos of it, probably too many.

It was like I had a new baby. I did everything but breast-feed it.

Because of the bees.

Ouchie.

At night, I went out and watched the butterflies flutter to

and fro. Bluebirds and wrens visited, and even two baby foxes came and tumbled around, adorably. I even took the time to smell the roses.

Literally.

They smelled great, and because the garden was right in front of my front door, its gentle fragrance wafted through the screen door.

In other words, it was all rainbows and sunshine, like *My Little Pony* but without the Pony.

I emailed one of my friends a garden photo, and she replied, "What about the deer?"

But I wasn't worried. I figured the deer were too busy eating the apples from my apple tree, so I figured they wouldn't bother my garden. Also, I always felt as if I had an understanding with the deer, since I like them and don't allow hunting at all.

I even saved a fawn once, whom I named Fawn Hall.

And I love Bambi.

So you know where this is going.

I woke up one morning, and my garden was green.

But only green.

No more rainbow, no more colors, no more sweetness and light. There were almost no flowers at all. I went outside in disbelief, and the garden consisted of leafy sticks. Deer had eaten most of the flowers.

Okay, I should have known.

But I didn't. When people complained about deer, I thought they were exaggerating.

And my first impulse was to kill deer, as many as possible.

Just kidding.

Mother Nature 1, Scottoline 0.

I calmed myself down, went to the store, and got a bottle of deer repellant made by a company called I Must Garden. I sprayed it on the stalks not because I Must Garden, but because I Must Win.

Or because I Am Smarter Than Deer.

Or because I Worked Too Hard on This Stupid Garden to Stop Now.

I never knew how deer repellent works and figured it was some mysterious alchemical mixture.

Wrong again, rookie.

I read the label and learned that it was "all natural," made of: "Putrescent whole egg solids, garlic, clove oil, and white pepper."

In other words, now I have a garden of green stalks that smells like garbage, topped with Caesar dressing.

No more lovely floral fragrance wafting into the house. I closed the door and dead-bolted it, to keep out the stench.

I may duct-tape the windows.

Mother Nature 2, Scottoline 0.

Enter more Nature, in the form of weeds.

By the way, deer don't eat weeds.

Thanks, Bambi.

And when I say weeds, I mean weeds, and tons of them. They sprouted everywhere through the mulch allegedly purposed to keep them down.

So now I get to go outside and weed like crazy. I can't tell the weeds from the plants, except that there are way more weeds than plants, and everything in the garden smells like puke.

Game, set, and match to Mother Nature.

# Make It Twerk

---

By Francesca

The word "twerking" was just added to Merriam-Webster's dictionary.

Does that mean I have to acknowledge it's a real thing?

I hate twerking. I hate the word. I hate the motion. I hate the craze.

I'd like to claim, and often do, that this is some sort of feminist stance. But I fear the real reason I hate twerking is more petty:

I can't do it.

I secretly consider myself a pretty great dancer. That's a risky thing to put in print, because I have zero training or recognizable dance skills to back it up. I'm sure there are small children on TLC who could put me to shame. My sole qualifications are that I fully commit, have a blast, and I *think* I can throw down. For most dancing scenarios, that's really all you need.

If you approach a dance move with the attitude, "mm-hm, watch this!" I guarantee you will execute it well enough to delight those around you. Dancing is simply the result of too much positive energy to remain standing, so don't let anything kill the buzz.

I've never been a shrinking violet on the dance floor. In

college, I didn't do a single drug, and I never once blacked out or vomited from alcohol. Instead, I danced on tables with little to no prodding. I could do it completely sober. During my freshman year, if you turned up the music, no elevated surface was safe.

I had somehow missed the slut-shaming memo that this was a "bad" thing to do. To me it seemed perfectly reasonable, even prudent. I could dance and have fun while staying safely out of reach of drunk guys and their grabby hands.

I took playing hard to get literally and made myself hard to reach.

How was I supposed to know this was the international symbol of train-wreck party girls the world over?

Eventually, I succumbed to societal pressure/gravity and put my table-dancing days behind me, but I'm not ashamed.

As Rizzo said, there are worse things I could do.

So I can't blame my morals for keeping me from twerking. Nor could anyone accuse me of lacking twerk-ethic. Believe me, I've spent some time in front of my bedroom mirror trying to get it. But my booty doesn't achieve that independent, lava-lamp jiggle. Instead, my butt does some sort of mechanical up-down motion, as if Disney's "It's a Small World" ride took you through the Red Light district.

Plus, I get tired.

And I'm bummed!

I want to be able to twerk and *then* reject it on principle, not the other way around. Twerking challenges my self-view, so it's only logical that I hate it.

This isn't the first time my dance-star illusions have been dispelled. I remember the night my new boyfriend casually mentioned that his ex-girlfriend was a dancer.

Modern dancing, that is, so you can't even snark it.

Normally I'm a paragon of well adjustment when it comes

to my significant others' ex-flames; the past is past, and I don't let it get to me. But something about her being a professional dancer brought up more insecurity for me than usual.

My best friend completely understood. "A dancer? Ugh, that's the worst! I'd rather she was in MENSA."

I'm fit, but I don't have a hard body by any definition. And I am comically inflexible; I worked up to touching my toes last year. Until that moment, it had never occurred to me to feel bad about these deficiencies. Sex is best done lying down for a reason, folks.

But if my boyfriend dated a dancer, I feared he might be into freaky, Cirque du Soleil stuff in bed—spins and tumbling and French people in funny hats and . . . clowns.

Thankfully, we agree on saving the clowns for special occasions.

Right around this time, a girlfriend of mine got me a gift certificate to attend a dance class for my birthday. She said the class was beginner-friendly and the instructor was great. I was excited—I thought it would be a fun workout and a great way to get my groove back. I picked out a *Flashdance*-inspired outfit to wear, and we headed up to the dance studio in Midtown.

Well, guess what?

I sucked.

Like, unbelievably bad. My friend struggled, too, but not like I did. Everything the teacher demonstrated was too fast for me. My feet were not cooperating. I confused my left and my right. I turned around a beat too soon and faced everyone's back. I was so much worse than I thought. It was humiliating.

Choreographed dancing is nothing like shaking it on the dance floor. It's all counting and memorization; it felt more like math than like fun. I hated it. And I hated being bad at it.

But I stuck it out, huffing and puffing, trying my best. I had given up on attempting to follow the teacher and was mainly watching a tall brunette behind me in the mirror as she expertly executed every move.

During one of the teacher's all-too-rare breaks, I turned around to the girl and said, between my heaving breaths, "I just want to apologize that you have to stand near me, because I know I am terrible. It's super helpful for me to watch you, but I'm probably messing you up. You're really amazing."

She laughed and shook her head, even tossing her hair with rhythm. "No, you're fine. It's a hard routine. We've been working on it all month."

"Huh?"

Are you twerking kidding me?

I looked around at the other girls with new eyes. I wasn't defective; they just knew the routine already! This truth didn't make me any better of a dancer, but it did make me a little kinder to myself.

A few weeks later my boyfriend and I went to a wedding together for the first time. When dinner had been cleared and the DJ got going, he asked me if I wanted to dance. The thought did cross my mind—this is a guy who can call your bluff.

But then I figured, ah, twerk it.

We danced to every song the DJ played. I shimmied, I twirled, I snapped, I shook, we slow-danced, we swing-danced, we salsa-ed, we jumped, we bumped, we grinded, we electric-slided. After they played that last song, I all but collapsed into a dining chair, sweaty, exhausted, and happy beyond measure.

My boyfriend crashed next to me. "You," he said, catching his breath, "are a great dancer."

I shook my head. "Not really. I just try to have fun."

Without twerking.

# Gangrene Thumb

By Lisa

You may recall I mentioned earlier that I water my garden too much.

That problem is now solved.

Because I'm out of water.

Our story begins when I noticed that the water pressure in my house is low.

Hmm.

By the way, I have well water. We live like pioneers in our township, which has no police, fire, or garbage removal, though I don't have to sew the American flag.

Thanks, township!

Anyway, the water level in my well generally goes down when there's no rain, but it was getting worse and worse until I realized that something must be wrong in the springhouse.

If you don't know what a springhouse is, welcome to the club.

All I know is that it's a picturesque little shed that houses where the water comes up from the well. More than that I can't explain, because I have no understanding of how my spring-house works. I never go in there because it's damp, dark, and scary, like a basement on steroids.

I called the plumbers who specialize in wells and they

wanted me to show them the springhouse, so I was shamed into going in. Inside were strange black gauges, weird blue tanks, and two body-size open trays of water, which is the water I drink, evidently lying around all day and night, so that bugs, snakes, paramecium, and God-knows-what-else can swim around in it before it finds its way into the glass that I put to my parched lips.

Delicious.

The plumbers inspect the well and say that it's fine, so we all leave the springhouse and troop around the lawn to solve the mystery of why I have no water. You don't have to be Nancy Drew to notice that the grass in my front yard, near the garden, is surprisingly soggy.

Uh-oh.

So we go find the faucet for the garden hose, which is in the garage, and the plumbers guess that the pipe must be leaking under the garage, since it was never used until I put in this stupid garden. They say it must have been corroding, but the corrosion was holding it together.

Like me.

Anyway, we trace the leak backwards to the basement under the garage, which is another place I never go because it's damp, dark, and scary, like a springhouse on steroids.

As soon as we open the door, we see that the basement brims with water. Pieces of wood, broken glass, and kreplach float by.

Long story short, we call in the plumbers who specialize in flood damage and they use three pumps to pump the water out of the basement. They figure out where the leak is in the pipe, but also surmise it can't possibly be causing the soggy grass. In other words, I have two leaks in two pipes, caused by watering the garden!

Yay!

We call in a third set of plumbers who specialize in second

Lisa's gardening requires heavy machinery.

leaks, and these are the guys who put on their booties before going to work.

For a middle-aged woman, a plumber is a booty call.

They find the leak under the soggy lawn but are not sure exactly where. They explain that they will need to dig trenches and lay new water lines, and that an estimator will come out on Saturday to tell me how much my gardening hobby is going to cost me.

Obviously, I have a green thumb.

Dollar green.

So by Sunday night, as I write, my entire front lawn is a swamp.

The only dry spot is the garden, where the flowers left by the deer are dying of thirst.

# Reply Hazy, Try Again

---

By Francesca

We associate age with wisdom. "Heed the lessons of those who have come before" is common advice, and the word "sage" has never been used for someone below the age of seventy. My grandmother is one of the smartest women I know, and she has lived through quite a lot in her time, so I'll gladly take any advice she has to give me.

If I could only understand it.

I know oracles are supposed to be cryptic, but help me out here.

First off, she loves to ask about my boyfriend. Every time she and I speak on the phone, her first questions are about him. How is he doing? Where is he right now? Where is he performing next?

I'm her only grandchild, not having me as her favorite person is a breach of contract.

And it took me by surprise. My grandmother hasn't always shown such an interest in men that I've dated, just this one, and they've never even met. But my boyfriend is a musician and composer, and my grandmother was a songwriter in her youth, so I guess that's the connection for her.

Also, I wondered if she secretly wants to see me settled and

234 | Scottoline and Serritella

married. She's ninety years old now, and I worry she won't get to see my wedding if I don't hurry up. But I can't rush things—not with my family history.

My mother and father have each been divorced twice. Even my grandmother has been divorced twice!

I come from a long line of indecision.

I intend to break the curse. If the Red Sox could do it, so can I.

So every time my grandmother asked about my boyfriend, I tried to indulge her. I went out of my way to tell her how happy I was, to enumerate my boyfriend's wonderful qualities, to talk up his career—*anything* I could say to make myself sound as content and secure as possible and ease her mind. Then, out of the blue, she had a new declaration:

"You need to shop around."

Excuse me? "Well, I'm not rushing into anything yet, but we are exclusive."

"So don't tell him."

"Muggy!" And here I thought she loved him.

"Be free. You don't need a man. You have a lot to offer."

*Ah,* I started to put it together; maybe I went overboard with the boy-talk. My grandmother has always been very independent, she was a career woman when very few were, and she probably wants to instill that same self-reliance in me. I thanked her and told her not to worry.

And I stopped mentioning him when we talked on the phone.

But it wasn't long until my grandmother had a new reading on my relationship:

"Where is your boyfriend? He's never with you!"

"Wait, what? No, he is, I just . . ." I thought you didn't want to hear about him anymore.

You know, the problem might be the medium, I thought.

My grandmother has a hard time hearing me over the phone, and I have a hard time understanding her, so some things had to be getting lost in translation.

But then, last month, my grandmother was visiting at my mom's house, so I went down, too, to spend time with her. One night, we were all hanging out in the living room, watching *Raymond* and discussing dinner plans when, without any prompting, my boyfriend popped into her mind again. And this time, she didn't have any trouble making herself crystal clear.

"How much does he earn?" she said.

I laughed out of shock. "I wouldn't know. I'm his girlfriend, not his accountant."

"You don't *know*?" Her eyebrows bounced atop her peach-framed glasses.

"I don't worry about it, and neither should you. You know why? Because I make enough money myself," I said, hoping to jog her memory of our independent-woman talk. "And what's that expression you always say? *You marry for money, you earn every penny.*"

She nodded at her own sage wisdom. "That's true."

"Right, so I love him, and that's all that matters."

"Ahh." She waved her hand at my silly idea.

But wasn't it her idea first?

Thus I came back to New York after our visit, none the wiser. Recently, my grandmother happened to call me when I was with my boyfriend. So when she asked her usual question about how he was doing, I casually mentioned, "Oh, he's here right now."

"Let me talk to him," she said.

*Uh-oh.* Would she ask him about his bank balance, his plans for our future, his smothering love, or his absenteeism?

"She's hard to understand," I blurted out, as I handed him the phone. Hoping I could blame any untoward statement on her stroke.

They talked for a few minutes that felt like fifteen. I stepped away to give them privacy, but really, I was just too nervous to stand around for it.

When my boyfriend gave the phone back to me, it looked almost like he had a tear in his eye.

*Oh, God,* I thought. But I plastered on a hopeful smile. "What did she say?"

"She told me she loved me," he said, *verklempt.*

*Phew.* "Of course she does!" I cried, hugging him.

For now.

# Restaurant Wars

## By Lisa

I'm so excited about a new restaurant that just opened in a trendy part of Brooklyn. You know what's on the menu?

Silence.

You got it. I'm going, and I'm taking Mother Mary.

It's true. This new restaurant has rules, and one of the rules is that you're not allowed to talk in the restaurant.

This is an even better restaurant rule than my personal favorite, Employees Must Wash Hands Before Returning to Work.

The restaurant owner got the idea for a silent-dining restaurant after a trip he took to India, where he saw Buddhist monks eating breakfast without talking.

This is what comes from travel.

Or so I hear, because I don't travel.

I hate to travel.

In fact, if I travel, it's to a restaurant.

The owner of the restaurant says that, "The silence speaks for itself."

I agree. However, what the silence says is anybody's guess.

I think the silence has strongly held opinions on the government shutdown, Obamacare, and most importantly, whether these jeans make me look fat.

The chef at the restaurant says that they don't need talking because "there's such a strong energy in the room."

Wow!

I think I might go to Brooklyn and start talking to silence and energy.

I could *travel* to Brooklyn!

By the way, the menu at the restaurant is $40 per meal, which proves that silence is golden.

Or at least totally overpriced.

In case you're interested in going, the restaurant is called Eat, but I think it should be called Shut Up.

Or Shut Up and Eat, which was what Mother Mary used to say to me all the time, when I was little.

She also used to say: Shut Up and Go Clean Your Room.

Shut Up and Wipe That Smile off Your Face.

Shut Up and Get out of My Sight.

And my personal favorite, Watch Your Tone.

Meanwhile, silent dining is a great idea!

I know a lot of people I would happily go to dinner with if I didn't have to interrupt my eating to talk to them or worse, to listen to them.

Mainly my ex-husbands, Thing One and Thing Two.

In fact, both of my horrible marriages would have been improved if we could have eaten dinner in silence. Or better yet, if we could have pretended that our stony silence during dinner was somebody else's rule and not the state of our horrible marriage.

Actually, that's an exaggeration.

We did talk during dinner. I remember once I said, Pass the salt.

Does that count?

Probably not, because what I really meant was, Pass the arsenic.

Too dark?

Which gives me another idea, because I also read about another new restaurant called In The Dark, and the rule there is that you have to eat in total darkness.

Don't you want to bring your exes there?

I would, but I'd go further. I'd like to open a new kind of restaurant that combined the two ideas. In other words, where you had to eat in the dark and you weren't allowed to talk to the people you were with.

Wow!

Great idea, huh?

I might be onto something, right?

I swear, I'd still be married to Thing One and/or Thing Two if I never had to see them or talk to them.

I thought I had to get a divorce to avoid seeing or talking to them, but it turns out, all I had to do was take them to my new restaurant.

Who knew?

What a country!

# Greased Lightning

By Lisa

I'm a big fan of combinations, like soup-and-sandwich. Peanut butter-and-jelly. Spaghetti-and-meatballs.

You may detect a pattern.

Carbohydrates are the leitmotif.

Or maybe the heavy-motif.

One combination I never thought of is jeans-and-moisturizer. Lucky for women, marketing has thought of that for us!

You may have read the news story which reported that Wrangler is selling a line of jeans that embeds microcapsules of moisturizer in the fabric, which evidently explode on impact with your thighs and moisturize them.

I think this is an awesome idea. I often fantasize about things that would explode on impact with my thighs, such as Bradley Cooper.

It gives new meaning to the term thunder thighs.

The line of jeans is called Denim Spa, which is quite a combination, right there. Denim and Spa are two words I have never experienced together.

Like love-and-marriage.

But to stay on point, Wrangler markets three types of moisturizer jeans. One comes embedded with Aloe Vera and another with Olive Oil, but choosing between the two is a no-brainer for me. I wouldn't pick Aloe Vera, because she sounds like someone I went to high school with and I don't share jeans.

I'd leave the aloe alone.

Instead I'd pick the olive oil. If I added balsamic, those jeans would be delicious.

But only extra virgins can wear them.

Count me out.

Come to think of it, if I were going to infuse jeans with food, I would go with Cinnabons.

Extra frosting is more fun than extra virgin.

The moisturizer in the jeans lasts up to fifteen days, but Wrangler also offers a "reload spray" that you can squirt your pants with. I'm not sure I'd buy the spray. It would be cheaper to pour olive oil on my pants, like a salad. I'd dress them properly, before I got dressed.

But the third type of moisturizer jeans is my favorite, and it's called Smooth Legs.

I need Smooth Legs. I have only Scaly Legs and Hairy Legs, or a combination of the two, which is Scary Legs.

The amazing thing about the Smooth Legs jeans is that they not only moisturize your legs, they fight cellulite.

Wow!

According to the website, the way they do this is by a "special formula" embedded in the jeans, which contains "caffeine, retinol, and algae extract."

Which contains mayonnaise.

Why fight jeans that fight cellulite?

I wouldn't. I'd be scared. They can "reload." I wouldn't buy them without a background check.

If you ask me, fighting cellulite is a lot to ask from a pair of pants, much less clothing in general, and you've got to hand it to Wrangler, which charges a mere $150 for a pair of these hard-working jeans. That's only $75 per leg or approximately $.03 per cellulite dimple, if you have 2,928,474,747 dimples, like me.

In fact, I just got another 4,928,749, in the time you took to read that last sentence.

In my experience, cellulite comes only in packs of 4,928,749.

I wouldn't mind having a pair of pants that fought cellulite for me, which would be like having a lawyer for my butt.

This is because I don't spend any time fighting my cellulite. On the contrary, my cellulite and I have an arrangement. My cellulite agrees to stay on the back of my legs, thighs, and tushie, and I agree not to look at myself from behind.

This turns out to be easy. Because I always move forward and never look back.

Metaphor not included.

In truth, I've come to accept and enjoy my cellulite. I can amuse myself by playing connect the dots on my thighs or finding constellations on my butt. For example, my left rump sports not only the Big and Little Dippers, but also the Serving Spoon, the Soup Ladle, and the Cake Knife.

The best thing about the moisturizer jeans is that all that grease must make them easier to get on. But being menopausal, I might need more lubrication.

Like motor oil.

Come to think of it, I won't be buying the moisturizer dungarees.

They're not worth dung.

# Do the Meth

By Lisa

I'm not good at math, but neither is the government.

As I write this, our government is sputtering to a halt, expecting to shut down by the weekend. So by now you know the ending, like a spoiler for the TV show *Breaking Bad.*

Except the government show is called *Breaking Down.*

And it's not that good.

Allow me to suggest that it doesn't matter whether the government managed to stave off this most recent shutdown, because this won't be the last.

Our government is hooked.

On math, not meth.

Here's how government math works.

Remember when Congress was debating whether we should have a war in Syria? All the talk was whether we should or we shouldn't. Nobody in Washington was saying that we couldn't, because we didn't have the money.

Except for us, the grown-ups who pay mortgages, send kids to college, and still get our hair highlighted every two months.

Blond does not come cheap.

So here's my question: If we can't afford to keep the government running now, how could we have afforded a war in Syria two weeks ago?

I don't know the answer, but the question itself solves all our budget problems. Because obviously, if we need the government to find some money, all we need to do is have a war. So ipso fatso, we need more wars.

Not really, just pretend.

All we have to do is *say* we're going to have a war.

And cross our fingers behind our backs.

Because magically, if we say the money is going to be spent on a war, the government finds the money.

God-knows-where.

China.

The sky.

Money trees.

I suspect that's it, the money grows on trees. Why do you think I started gardening?

So here's the plan, and don't tell anyone, least of all the government.

(No worries, they never listen to us anyway.)

Let's say we're going to have a war and act like we mean it, like with Syria. Then, get a whole bunch of catcher's mitts and catch the money when the government shakes it from the trees. Finally, when we have all the money in a nice, big pile, let's say we changed our minds.

We'll say we're too busy to have a war.

We're too busy counting money.

Or we'll make up another excuse, like we're getting our hair highlighted.

Or we just can't come to the phone.

We're *busy*.

If that doesn't work, we have to start doing math as badly as

I do, which is still better than government math. Here's how to do Scottoline math:

Every time I see something I want, like a new dress, I ask myself:

Will it make me look thin?

No, sorry, not the point.

Let's try again: Every time I see something I want, like a new dress, I ask myself:

Will it make me look young?

Also off the point. Sorry, I got carried away from all the dress-shopping.

Truly, the first question I ask myself is:

Can I afford it?

Not, do I need it?

Not, do I want it?

Not, do I deserve it?

Can-I-afford-it is the first question I ask myself, and sometimes the last. If the answer is no, I don't get to the other questions. Because I obviously need, want, and deserve whatever it is.

I'm me! And it's for me! Who's to say no?

Me?

Under Scottoline math, it doesn't matter if the thing I want is a new dress or a new war. If I can't afford it, I can't afford it.

And if I wasn't broke two weeks ago, why am I broke now?

Because in the meantime, I didn't even buy the dress.

Pardon me, but I'm confused by my government.

But then again, I'm no meth whiz.

# Suing Stevie Wonder

### By Francesca

"I need to sue Stevie Wonder" is not a sentence you hear every day, certainly not out of the mouth of my ninety-year-old grandmother. But last week she called me and said just that.

I was in my apartment in New York when my grandmother called from Miami. Her first request was for my boyfriend's phone number. I asked her, "Why do you need his number?"

"To call him!" she cried, exasperated already, and we were only forty-five seconds into the call. "I need to speak to him as a musician."

My boyfriend happens to have a soft spot for grannies, and while I was sure he would happily take the call, I know my grandmother well enough to smell trouble.

"He's playing an out-of-town gig today and is hard to reach. Why don't you tell me what's going on and maybe I can help."

She sighed, then laid it on me, matter-of-fact. Her speech and voice have been compromised by past decades of smoking, throat-cancer treatment, and several strokes, so at first I assumed I misheard her. But she repeated it:

"I need to sue Stevie Wonder for copyright infringement. He stole my song."

Oh, dear.

I had been warned by my mother and uncle that this was the latest of my grandmother's quasi delusions. By way of background, my grandmother was a songwriter in the fifties and sixties and victim of one legitimate instance of copyright infringement, when one of her songs was stolen and used in a Tony-award-winning musical. (We'll let it remain nameless so that they don't come sue us.) But her claim was apparently legitimate enough that the musical's creators offered to settle.

My grandmother, however, has never been one to settle easily.

She rejected their cash offer on principle. She wanted her day in court.

But she underestimated just how much suing someone costs. And she'd have to go to New York to do it? Are you kidding? Nothing ever happened.

Not that the thieves got away with it—the Italian powers of the Evil Eye are almost as damaging as a jury verdict.

So as we spoke on the phone now, I had a hunch that this current legal concern of hers was some mixed-up memory of the past. But I tried to take it seriously and reason with her. "Muggy, it would be very difficult to sue Stevie Wonder."

"How do you know?" she snapped.

"Remember my dad? He's a copyright lawyer, so I know how this works."

"Good. Then I need your father's phone number."

"I'll tell you what, I'll ask him about it and get back to you, okay?"

I heard Uncle Frank calling to her in the background, asking who was on the phone. She ignored him and said to me, "Just because I am old, doesn't mean I can't fight for my rights!"

*Ugh,* that broke my heart.

She must have handed the phone to my uncle, because his

voice popped on the line. "Is this the Stevie Wonder stuff again? It's all she'll talk to anyone about. I don't know where she got the crazy idea."

I told him she wanted to call my dad.

"MA!" he yelled to her from the phone, this time at close range to my eardrum. "We can't call Lisa's *ex-husband!*"

As if that were the craziest part of my grandmother's request.

"He probably wouldn't mind." My dad also has a soft spot for my grandmother but . . .

"No," Frank said. "It'll only make it worse. She has to let this go."

I agreed and said good-bye.

But even though I thought it was as ridiculous as my uncle did, I had told my grandmother I would get back to her, and it didn't sit well with me not to honor my promise. So I called my dad at work and told him I just needed some official-sounding statement to help my grandmother move on. But my dad, never one to turn down a legal riddle, was intrigued. So I gave him all the details that she had told me, and my father gave her case the full workup over the phone, *pro bono.*

I called my grandmother right away. "Well, I spoke to my dad, and I got an answer. I don't think it's the one you want, but I hope this can give you some closure." I had Uncle Frank's warning in my head, and I was afraid to upset her with the bad news. Especially as I didn't know how much she'd be able to understand, between her hearing problems and the legalese. But I had come this far, so I spoke slowly and deliberately and hoped for the best.

I explained that in order to establish legitimate copyright infringement, one has to demonstrate both a significant similarity *and* probable access to the original work by the offending party. Since her song was written and recorded in 1960, and Wonder's was in 1984, probable access was highly improbable.

Mary Scottoline's songs didn't get quite the airplay as Stevie Wonder's.

"I don't think Stevie Wonder stole it intentionally, but I own the copyright so I want to sue his publishing company," my grandmother clarified.

So much for not knowing what she's talking about.

But alas, I had to tell her that if Wonder wrote his song without hearing hers, his separate copyright was protected by "independent creation," which allows for two artists to coincidentally create similar work. And there is a statute of limitations on the time between discovery, when my grandmother first noticed the similarity between the songs, and her opportunity to litigate, so, considering Wonder's song was a huge hit in the '80s, it would be hard to argue that that window hadn't closed. And finally, since her copyright was granted in 1960 and never renewed, it had doubtlessly expired.

"I know it's not what you wanted to hear, Muggy, and I'm sorry to disappoint you. But I want you to know that I took it very seriously, and I respect you too much not to tell you the truth."

My grandmother remained silent on the line, highly uncharacteristic.

I was sure I overwhelmed her. "Are you okay?"

"Yes," she said, finally. "Thank you very much. I am satisfied."

I was shocked. And then I kicked myself for underestimating her.

It was like she said; just because she's old, doesn't mean she can be dismissed. Who are we to be her judge and jury? Because in a family, unlike a court of law, there's no statute of limitations on being heard. In a family, you can air your grievances, however crazy they may sound. I was glad my grandmother felt listened to and could finally put the matter to rest.

And, Stevie Wonder, you can thank me later.

# Ho for the Burn

By Lisa

I couldn't be more excited about two new fitness crazes—exercising in high heels and/or on a stripper pole.

I can't think of a better message for young girls than exercising is important, but only if you look pornographic.

Obviously, whoever said women couldn't achieve equality in athletics had no idea what they were talking about.

Or maybe it's called a craze because it's crazy.

We begin with Heel Hop, which is an hour-long workout, including sit-ups, stretches, and lunges, but you do all the exercises wearing high heels.

Don't forget your stilettos—and Blue Cross card.

The instructor is a backup dancer named Kamilah, who says, "I came straight out of the womb with some high-heeled pumps."

I have one word for Kamilah:

Ouch.

I wish I knew Kamilah's mother, so I could give her a big hug—and a Bronze Star.

I'm hoping Kamilah doesn't start a new craze among fetuses, who will begin demanding high-heeled pumps in the womb. Because we don't need babies making their exit—or their entrance, depending on how you look at it—in even an infant-size pair of heels.

Unless you want to save the doctor fees on your episiotomy.

But that's not where I'd cut costs.

No pun.

I read online that Heel Hop is taught in classes held in Los Angeles.

I know, it makes you want to move to Los Angeles.

And if you do, you should. Move there. And stay there. Go away and never come back. I don't want to run into you in the market.

I'll be the one in muddy clogs.

The article I read about Heel Hop contained an interview with a podiatrist. They asked him about working out in high heels, and he said, "Exercising in them just doesn't make sense in any way, shape, or form."

But what does he know?

He's only a doctor, not a dancer, and therefore unqualified to give an opinion.

I bet he can't even walk in heels.

In fact, I challenge him to pronounce Louboutin.

Hint: Louboutin is French for you're-gonna-break-your-ankle.

But an even better fitness craze is exercising on a stripper pole, which I saw on one of the *Real Housewives* reality shows, where the housewives were taking lessons, spinning around the pole.

I'm sure this is exactly your reality, spending your free time spinning around poles with your girlfriends.

Of course that's not reality.

Real women don't have free time.

In any event, you'll be happy to know that you can find lots of DVDs online that will teach you how to work out on a stripper pole. I like the website called FlirtyGirlFitness, which says, "Treadmills, bench presses, and stair climbers have been replaced with dance poles, kitchen chairs, and pink feather boas."

This may be news to Nike.

I bet right now they're figuring out a way to paste a swish onto a boa.

Maybe they should just paste it onto a pastie.

Buy two.

Also I'm wondering what FlirtyGirlFitness is doing with their kitchen chairs. I need mine for sitting on while I eat chocolate cake.

The problem with exercising on a pole is that you need to install a pole in your house, which could be embarrassing when it comes time to sell. Unless you convince potential buyers that you're a fireman.

And think about what happens when you abandon your pole exercises, as you inevitably will. A pole isn't like a treadmill, in that you can't leave your dirty clothes on it. They'll fall right off.

I don't buy exercise equipment that I can't use for a hamper.

But amazingly, FlirtyGirlFitness has an answer for what to do with your abandoned pole. The website says that their poles come with "a special hook that will allow you to use this space to hang a plant."

How's that for a sales pitch?

Ladies, now you can combine your love of gardening with your need to look like a hooker!

I'm sure there's a market for that, and it's born every minute.

I just hope it wears flats.

# Magic Kingdom

---

By Lisa

It's the rich versus the handicapped.

Guess who's winning.

Bingo.

I read it in the paper.

The first incident I read about took place in Newport, Rhode Island, where there are stately mansions owned by families like the Vanderbilts, who got here a long time before the Scottolines.

The Vanderbilts came over on the *Mayflower,* in contrast to my ancestors, who took the bus.

With about ten transfers.

Anyway, according to the news story, lots of tourists go see the mansions in Newport, so many that somebody proposed to build a visitor center with handicapped-accessible ramps and bathrooms. This idea evidently caused the rich people in Newport to write letters opposing the visitor center, and in particular, the gift shop.

That's un-American.

I can't imagine anybody being opposed to a gift shop.

Everybody knows that the best part of any attraction is the gift shop.

You can go to any art museum, fancy mansion, or pretzel factory, and the best time you will have is in the gift shop.

Where else can you flatten a copper penny?

When Daughter Francesca was little, her favorite part of the zoo was the gift shop, which came at the end. She loved the monkeys, giraffes, and the eagle named Kippee, but throughout the entire zoo, she would talk about the punchball she would get in the gift shop.

And by talk, I mean whine.

In time I figured out that it would be smarter to take her to the gift shop first, so that she got her punchball right off the bat. Then we got a membership to the zoo, to go for free, and we would skip the animals altogether and go only to the gift shop.

Whatever, giraffes.

Long necks. We get it.

To return to point, evidently Gloria Vanderbilt didn't appreciate the need for a gift shop or a bathroom, much less one that's accessible to the handicapped. She called the mansions a "magical kingdom" and opposed having a handicapped-accessible visitor center because she didn't want a "new building selling plastic shrink-wrapped sandwiches."

Obviously, this is the epitome of discrimination.

Against shrink-wrapped sandwiches.

Shrink-wrapped sandwiches are the equal of any other sandwich.

I would think that a woman as classy as Gloria Vanderbilt could look beyond the wrapping to the content of the sandwich, but no.

So let's review.

Thus far, the rich people are winning.

The handicapped are holding it in.

And triangular tuna sandwiches don't stand a chance.

The second incident I read about takes place at the real Magic Kingdom, where the handicapped strike back against the rich.

But they still don't win.

It turns out that rich people at Disneyland have been taking advantage of the park's practice to let handicapped people go to the head of the line.

The handicapped get all the breaks, don't they?

If you had a million bucks, you could see how waiting in line would burn you up. You'd have to stand in the lovely California sunshine, spend time with your family, and listen to your kids talk.

And by talk, I mean whine.

Anyway, time is money, and no one knows that better than rich people, who reportedly started paying random handicapped people $1,000 a day to tell the Disneyland officials that they were part of the family, so that the rich people could get to the front of the line.

If you ask me, that's win-win.

The rich people get to go to the head of the line. And the handicapped people get to push them off Space Mountain.

To digress a moment, I've had a lot of strange jobs in my broke days. I volunteered for focus groups, I waited tables, I even practiced law.

So yes, I can be bought.

But you couldn't pay me enough to steer rich people around Disneyland and pretend they were my family.

Okay, maybe I would.

But I would not take them on the It's A Small World exhibit more than one time. You couldn't pay me enough. When Daughter Francesca was little, she wanted to go on that exhibit four times in a row. Of course, I took her.

I didn't even charge her.

Also she was only five years old, and I don't think she was good for it.

But I read that Disneyland has just suspended the practice of letting the handicapped go to the front of the line, even though it was making money for handicapped people willing to hang out with rich people who would teach their kids it's okay to lie if it gets you to the front of the line.

Who was handicapped, again?

# A Wall of Guilt

---

## By Francesca

"I think he swallowed it," my boyfriend said, his eyes full of worry.

"The whole thing?" My heart dropped.

My little dog was in trouble.

It had begun as one of those perfect early-summer days. My boyfriend and I had taken the train with my dog, Pip, in tow to a friend's Memorial Day barbecue. On the way there, I had been so charmed by how cute my two favorite boys looked together—Pip's adorable face popping out of his travel bag from underneath my boyfriend's arm—I'd snapped a picture.

Now my boyfriend was telling me that Pip had swallowed an entire cooked chicken leg bone.

"I gave it to him to chew and looked away for a second, and it was gone. I just thought he would chew on it, I never thought he would eat it," my boyfriend said in a rush of words. "Is that bad?"

A lot went through my head at that moment. A lifetime of owning dogs had ingrained the cardinal rule that you can never give a dog a cooked bone. I knew that chicken bones in particular splinter inside a dog's body and can wreak havoc on the intestines. I knew that my dog's small size would not work in his favor. I knew that I loved Pip as if he were my own child. But the face across from me was one I also loved, and he looked stricken—and he didn't even know how bad it was.

So I swallowed it.

"It can be," I said with false calm. "No need for alarm, but I do need to make some calls right now to take care of this."

I left him in the yard and asked the host of the party for the number of a local emergency vet. In a private room down the hall, I spoke with the vet's receptionist. I also called my friend who just graduated from vet school. All of the advice was that if he already swallowed it, it was too late. They couldn't get the bone up without possibly damaging the dog's throat. There was nothing to do but wait and see if he got sick, and if he did, he might need surgery. I called my mom.

When my boyfriend came looking for me, I hung up the phone.

"Are you okay?" he asked, concerned.

"Oh, yeah. They say just to keep an eye on him."

"I'm so sorry, babe."

"Don't worry about it. I don't blame you at all." That was the truth. It was an accident. Pip could have just as easily eaten it off the trash or off another guest's plate. I didn't care how Pip got the bone in his body; all that mattered was that we get it out.

And I knew my boyfriend loved Pip, but he never had a dog growing up, so he didn't know what they can and can't eat. Most of all, I knew my boyfriend felt terrible. And I didn't want him to feel any more guilty.

It was much easier to focus on my own guilt.

My mind circled over all of my own lapses that led to Pip being able to eat the bone. I never let him off the leash, but the yard was fenced and some of the guys at the party wanted to play fetch with Pip. I'm usually sitting next to my boyfriend, but I wanted to have some girl time, so I wasn't at his table. I'm always so careful with Pip.

Until I wasn't.

On the train home, my dog and my boyfriend fell asleep leaning on me. I stayed awake, worrying.

As much as I needed comfort and reassurance, I didn't feel like I could ask for it from him. Because to ask for it would be to confess how scared I was and how devastated I would be if something were to happen, and I didn't want to make him feel any worse. But he wouldn't leave my side. I spoke to my mother on the phone in clipped sentences and optimistic intonation to hide her worried reaction on the other line.

And to hide my own.

I went into the bathroom and cried silently into my hands.

It wasn't sitting well with me, this whole "watch and wait" advice I had gotten earlier. I made Pip a special dinner of boiled chicken and rice and pumpkin filling to help him pass anything easily. I considered calling the ER vet in my area, but what was the emergency? We had already gotten an answer, it was late at night now, and I was probably being paranoid.

I didn't mention my concerns to my boyfriend.

Instead, we watched a movie on TV, as we had planned to earlier in the day. Or rather we both looked in the direction of the TV while a movie played. Both our minds were elsewhere.

The next morning, we went about our usual routine, walking Pip to a nearby coffee shop, but my boyfriend stayed about three paces ahead or behind me.

I asked him what was wrong, even though I knew.

"I just can't believe it. This is all my fault."

"Anyone could've given him the bone."

"But anyone didn't. I did."

I could see him beating himself up. "Hey, don't do that to yourself. I told you, I don't blame you at all. But I need your support right now. You can't pull away just because you feel bad," I said, even as I knew that I had been doing exactly the same thing.

He nodded, but the space between us remained.

After breakfast I reassured him I was fine and encouraged him to go home. He told me to keep him updated as to how Pip was feeling and left.

As soon as he was out the door, I called the vet hospital I would normally go to in my area and explained the situation, asking if they thought I should bring him in.

"When did this happen?" the vet tech asked over the phone.

"Yesterday afternoon."

"I wish you had brought him in right when it happened. We have more options the sooner we get to the dog. But yes, bring him right away."

I hung up the phone and bawled. Had I not pursued Pip's care as aggressively as I would have because I was trying to protect my boyfriend's feelings? Had I denied my own gut instinct? And was my dog about to pay for it?

The thought alone ripped me in two.

I called my mom again.

"Are you by yourself?" she asked. "Why don't you have him go with you?"

But I didn't want my boyfriend to come. I wanted to be alone so that in case I got bad news, I could have whatever reaction I needed to, even if it was hysterical.

The way I saw it, he couldn't make it any better, so why make him feel worse?

I needed to deal with it by myself.

But once at the vet's office, all that pent-up emotion was busting out at the seams. I teared up telling the vet tech simple things like Pip's age, weight, and whether he was neutered or not. I cried when I told the vet what happened. I cried as they took Pip in the back to be X-rayed.

At first I felt freedom in being alone. But after the initial relief of letting some emotion out and sitting in the waiting area, I just felt . . . lonely.

There was another woman in the waiting room, calling attention to herself by raising her voice at the vet, who was clearly trying to keep the conversation in lower tones. I caught the drift that they were waiting on blood-test results, but the vet was not optimistic as to her older dog's prognosis. The woman was not taking it well. She was being rude, in a way, but I could see she was panicked. I saw other people in the waiting room turn away out of embarrassment.

The vet left and the woman took a seat not far from mine. She began crying noisily.

By herself.

There was a box of tissues on the side table next to me and I brought them over to her. I asked if she was all right.

Her words rushed out like a dam had broken. Her toy poodle was fourteen years old. She knew the dog had a heart condition, but her regular vet was unavailable for the holiday, and now this new vet thought she should put the poodle down. She's been living out of hotels because her apartment has black mold, and this little dog goes everywhere with her. It sleeps on her head. She said she couldn't sleep without it. The dog was her sole companion.

And it sounded to me like she was going to have to say goodbye.

"I've never killed one of my dogs before," she said, blowing her nose.

I knew I couldn't make her situation any better, but I talked to her anyway. I got her a cup of water from the cooler to help calm her down. I assured her that the vets were only trying to help and offer their expert opinion, but that ultimately she had to make the decision she felt comfortable with. I told her about the times I had to put a pet down, and how it can be loving and peaceful.

I identified with her, and how important her pet was to her. But then I realized, she didn't have anyone else there to comfort her, while I was alone by choice.

They called my name at the desk, and I went back to the examining room. The vet was tacking up the X-ray results on the light board, but they hadn't brought Pip up. I braced for the worst.

"Well, we took four different angles on him—he's a very sweet boy, very cooperative—and I don't see any bone."

I was stunned. But he explained to me that any bone particles would show up white, and there were none. I asked him to double-check that it was the right dog, but it was true. No bone. Either it was a false alarm or the power of prayer works.

Then a tech walked in with my Pip, his tail wagging like crazy. I scooped him up and kissed him, thanking everyone in sight.

On my way out, I hugged the woman waiting on her poodle and wished her the best. She seemed steadier.

With the crisis averted, I saw my own behavior in greater clarity. Both of our guilt—his for making an honest mistake, mine at the prospect of communicating my fear and making him feel worse—completely got in the way of us leaning on each other. If I had asked my boyfriend to come with me, he would have. Even if he couldn't fix it, he might have made me feel better. And we could have gone through it together.

I learned that protecting someone by keeping him away from me doesn't shelter either of us. I learned that feeling other people's feelings for them doesn't bring us closer, it only separates me from myself and my needs. I always thought being codependent meant being too emotionally glued to someone; I didn't realize the way I was doing it was setting me adrift.

I called my boyfriend and told him the good news. We were both relieved and elated.

"So when can you come over?"

# Mrs. Uncle Sam

---

By Lisa

I found the perfect man for Mother Mary:

Uncle Sam.

Why not?

They'd be great for each other. Uncle Sam may be over two hundred years old, but he's got plenty of life left in him. After all, we found out that he sicced the IRS on Tea Party groups and spied on a hundred AP reporters.

In other words, he's an active senior.

A *very* active senior.

Or maybe a hyperactive senior.

But still, he's just the type of man that Mother Mary needs. He's tall, handsome, and he spends money like there's no tomorrow.

By the way, did I mention there's no tomorrow?

I smell New Daddy.

And because I know a good man is hard to find, I'm not going to be too picky about him. In fact, I did some research on the Tea Party business, and while it bothers me, it would be worse if he went after the Coffee Party.

Or the Chocolate Cake Party.

Then the party would be over.

Also I read about what he did to the Tea Party people. When they applied for tax-exempt status, he sent them lots of red tape.

Miles and miles of red tape.

Obviously, Uncle Sam keeps a lot of red tape on hand and maybe he just got carried away.

He does that all the time.

Like when he goes shopping, he doesn't worry about price. I heard he paid five hundred bucks for a screwdriver once. Obviously, he likes screwdrivers and he gets carried away easy.

He has no governor, for a government.

Anyway, back to the red tape. Maybe Uncle Sam mistook it for red ribbon. Maybe he thought he was wrapping gifts for the Tea Party.

Lots and lots of gifts.

He must really like tea.

You have to consider that Uncle Sam apologized for sending the red tape to the Tea Party, and that counts in his favor. Mother Mary needs a man who will say he's sorry.

Because he will be.

If he brings flowers, Mother Mary will become Mrs. Uncle Sam.

I also looked into that business with the reporters. It turns out that Uncle Sam secretly got the records for twenty different phone lines that belonged to Associated Press, which included the cell, office, and home phones of about a hundred reporters.

See what I mean?

He's crazy active.

Just because he's older, he's not sitting around on his duff. He's busy getting phone records.

Hundreds and hundreds of phone records.

You have to put what he did in context, and I read that Uncle Sam got the records to find a leak. So Uncle Sam is handy, and who doesn't like that in a man?

Plus, you know how hard it is to find a leak?

I have a leak in my kitchen celling, and it's really a problem. I've called plumber after plumber but none of them can find the leak, much less stop it. One had a small videocamera that came on a long hose and he stuck that in the pipe, but even he couldn't find the leak.

At least Uncle Sam didn't use the camera hose on the reporters.

Ouch.

The plumbers charged me a fortune to find the leak, but Uncle Sam didn't charge the AP reporters anything at all. He got their phone records for free.

What a guy!

So are you with me, should we put those two crazy kids together?

Maybe Uncle Sam will take her name.

Mr. Mother Mary.

# Mother Mary Twerks It Out

---

## By Lisa

This weekend I had 1,000 people over. And Mother Mary. Guess which put me over the top.

Just kidding.

We begin with some background. For eight years now, I've been giving a book club party at my house, for book club members who read my Spring hardcover.

Yes, you read that right.

If your book club reads my April book, and you email or send me a picture of everyone holding the book up, then you're invited to the book club party at my house. Daughter Francesca speaks, Amazing Assistants Laura and Nan speak, and I speak, and you get the idea. We have you all over, feed you, and yak at you for an afternoon.

I believe I am the only author on the planet who does this.

Because I'm just crazy enough.

Security risk?

I pray not. Also I have an excellent security system.

Five yapping dogs.

Really, any evildoer will get the biggest headache of his life.

. . .

When we started the book club party, we had it for one day and we hosted almost a hundred people. We served homemade chocolate chip cookies, which were underdone, and plugged in coffee urns that blew every fuse in the house.

But a good time was had by all.

Happily, the book club party has grown to 1,000 people over two days, and we keep it to 500 a day, because that keeps us in brownies.

Brownies are the life of every girl party.

And now there's a wait list, which makes me just as happy as a bestsellers list.

Thank you, dear readers!

This year, the book party was special because it fell so close to Mother Mary's 90th birthday, which was a huge milestone.

For me.

I have lived with her all my life, which feels like 90 years.

Again, just kidding.

Mother Mary loves coming up for the book club party, because it's her chance to tell everyone that I'm a pain in the ass.

So this time I thought celebrating her birthday would be an added bonus for everyone, especially Mother Mary, who would have 1,000 new friends to sing Happy Birthday to her. But no, she said, when I asked her.

"Ma, you don't want to have the book club people sing Happy Birthday to you?"

"No."

"Why not?"

"I said no."

"But it will be so much fun. These people have read about you and they would love to celebrate you, and so would I. I'll get you a nice cake."

"No."

"Ma, it's a very big deal, turning ninety. Not everyone gets that chance."

"No."

"What if I have somebody jump out of the cake?"

Mother Mary lifts an eyebrow. "Who?"

"Telly Savalas."

"He's dead."

"My point exactly!"

"I. Said. No." Mother Mary scowled, which is her default expression. As she gets older, she has come more into herself, which is Yosemite Sam on blood thinners.

But you know where this is going, because possession is nine-tenths of the law. I was hoping that once I had her in my clutches, I would get my own way, because the only way I can ever get my way with my mother is if she's captured and caged. Then I figured I would wheel her out in front of the cake, on a dolly like Hannibal Lecter.

Happy Birthday, Mommy!

And when I picked her and Brother Frank up at the airport, my optimism soared because she was so cooperative. Case in point, she arrived as usual in her white lab coat, but she agreed not to wear it to the party because it had a tomato stain from the Bloody Mary she had on the plane.

Surely, you have these problems in your own family. I bet your aged parents spill drinks on their Halloween costumes, too.

Anyway, to fast-forward, she came to the book club party with Brother Frank, climbed up on the little stage, and said hello to the crowd.

Then she refused to give up the microphone.

She told jokes, showed off her back scratcher, and twerked, AARP-style.

And she didn't even curse at me when we brought out the birthday cake.

Francesca dolls up Mother Mary for her birthday celebration.

Every single person sang Happy Birthday to her, and there wasn't a dry eye in the place. I know that some of the people were thinking of her, and some were thinking of their own mothers, whom they weren't so lucky to have around anymore.

Ninety Years of Mother Mary.

To me, it's still not enough.

# My Grandmother Is Not the Same

By Francesca

My grandmother is not the same.

It's not something I allow myself to say often, and I wouldn't want her to know I thought so, but it's true. She's going to be ninety years old in two weeks, so I guess I should've expected changes.

But we never expect our loved ones to change. They are the rocks, the solid foundation upon which we build our lives. For my entire life, I have defined my grandmother by the way she is feisty, willful, contrary, and irrepressible.

In other words, not all that open to change. She's not exactly known for her wiggle room.

But the last several years have been hard on my grandmother; she battled and won a fight against throat cancer, and she's suffered a heart attack and strokes. Whenever someone asks me how she's doing, I say something like, "Great! She's still her old self! No keeping her down!" or, "You know how she is. Cancer shouldn't mess with *her!*"

It's what I told myself.

But while her resilience has been an absolute marvel, I know her struggles have taken their toll. Talking—always my grandmother's favorite pastime and greatest liability—has become difficult for her. She works with a speech therapist to get her smack talk back up to speed, but it's been hard to get the words to match that wit.

I know all of this, but I try not to think about it.

So when I heard she was coming to visit last month, all I thought of was how excited I was to see her. Last year, she wasn't well enough to travel, but this year she wanted to come up and celebrate her ninetieth birthday with all of us. She was at my mom's house for three weeks, and I came down from New York so as not to miss a day with her.

There has never been a time that my grandmother visited and we didn't cook together, and I didn't want this visit to be any different. We decided on eggplant parmigiana, a perennial favorite in our family.

And a particularly good choice for my grandmother, because ever since she had radiation on her throat, she can only eat soft foods and finds most pastas too chewy.

We got the family all together in the kitchen: My grandmother was installed in a chair at the island, the catbird seat for recipe supervision; my uncle Frank was helping to organize the ingredients; my mother manned the bubbling tomato sauce; and I stood at the stove, frying the eggplant slices.

I've learned and relearned these recipes over the years, so much that I even make them at home for friends now. But making them on my own isn't as special as making them with my grandmother. It's more fun to do as a family, and my grandmother always coos over me.

But this time I couldn't do anything right.

"Looks good, doesn't it?" I said, showing my grandmother the growing pile of golden brown fried eggplant.

"No," my grandmother said.

"No? What's wrong with it?"

"Not dark enough." Her speech was halting, as if the "d" in "dark" got caught in her throat.

"Ma, they're perfect, she's doing a great job," my mom said in my defense. "You don't want her to burn them."

"Not burnt, brown!" My grandmother was angry now, and the words were almost indistinguishable. She has always been quick to sass you, but quick to anger was new.

The eggplant was cooked to the exact shade of toasty brown we've always made them. I have the timing down perfectly, three minutes in the oil each side, just like she taught me. The only possible explanation was that she couldn't see them clearly. Her eyesight has gotten much worse, and she can no longer read type or see most pictures in a magazine.

"But they are brown, Muggy," I said as gently as possible, trying to think of an excuse for her. "I bet it's the light over the oven that's making them look lighter."

My grandmother frowned. "How 'bout the sauce?"

"You want to taste it? Hang on, here I come." I cupped my hand beneath the wooden spoon and brought it over to where she was seated.

But when she reached for the spoon, her hands shook. Her face twisted in frustration and she banged her fist on the table.

"It's okay, Muggy," I said, using my pet name for her. "Take your time." I remembered my uncle's warning about her "intention tremors," shaking that comes on with volitional movement, like reaching. But seeing the tremor wasn't nearly as troubling to me as it was to see her upset.

My grandmother shot me a look from over her glasses, as if to say, "Can you believe this s--t?"

"I'll help you hold it, okay? Try again."

Her hand steadied this time, and the sauce was approved.

My mother caught my eye as she went over to my grandmother. "Ma, I think you're tired. Why don't you take a nap now? You can rest while we finish up."

But Muggy waved her off. She wanted to stay and make sure we didn't mess anything else up.

We ran into trouble again after I had finished frying the eggplant. I brought the heaping plate of them over to the kitchen island to begin assembling the stacks in the casserole dish.

"Did you count them?" my grandmother asked.

Of course, I hadn't. We never did that, and it would be terribly tedious to do now. "No, why would I?"

"To make the sta—, the sta—" Her mouth was open, but the words weren't coming out. Suddenly she shut her mouth and she shook her head, frustrated again.

"Don't get upset." I was more than happy to wait. "You don't have to rush, I'm listening."

She took a breath and tried again. "To make them even."

"I'll make sure the stacks are even by keeping track of how many layers as I go along, okay?"

That seemed to satisfy her, but her unusually exacting directions continued. When my uncle began sprinkling shredded mozzarella on the first layer of eggplant, my grandmother, words failing her, rapped a spoon on the table.

"Ma, what?" he said.

Her wide eyes were magnified by her glasses as she glared at him. "Spoon!"

"My hands are clean, I just washed them."

She shook her head. "To measure."

I have never in my life seen my grandmother use conventional measuring tools. She has taught me how to make ravioli, ricotta gnocchi, tomato sauce, and the best meatballs I've ever tasted, and she has never measured a thing. Instead she cooks by look, taste, and above all, texture: They should look golden brown. It should not stick to the table. The knife should cut it cleanly. Season to taste.

The joy of Italian cooking is that it is *not* an exact science. You know who taught me that?

My grandmother.

My uncle said, "Mom, we have made this fifty times at home, we've never used a tablespoon to measure."

I knew he was right, and I suspect my grandmother did, too, but she wouldn't admit she had made a mistake. Either that, or perhaps she was just craving control when so many things in her life that we all take for granted—the power of speech, the ability to see, to swallow—were newly out of her control. Getting a recipe exactly right took on heightened importance.

I got a tablespoon to measure.

We finally managed to get the eggplant parm into the oven, but we were all a little more exhausted than I remember us being in the past. My grandmother finally went to take that nap.

Ironically, she slept through dinner and didn't have any eggplant at all.

It's not easy for me to adjust to my grandmother's changes, but it's a lot harder for her. I wish she would realize we don't mind being patient, and I wish she would be more patient with herself. There is no shame in letting us see the cracks in her tough-girl façade; she doesn't have to be tough with us.

Sometimes I catch myself looking away when she has a coughing fit, not because I don't want to see it, but because I don't want her to feel like I see it. I catch myself finishing her sentences for her when her speech falters, not because I can't wait, but because I don't want her to get frustrated. She's a proud woman, and I want to let her save face.

But that isn't helping.

What I need to show her is that I love her regardless, and that I can be patient regardless. Love, like Italian cooking, has a lot of give in it. We don't need to be exacting with the ones we love, there's wiggle room. And likewise, she doesn't need to worry so much. She can give up control, because we've learned the lessons she taught us so well. She built this family, and now I want her to take her time and enjoy it.

None of the changes in her make any difference in the way I feel about her. When it comes to my grandmother, the world can wait, as far as I'm concerned.

And Heaven, too.

# Acknowledgments

By Lisa and Francesca

We would like to express our love and gratitude to everyone at St. Martin's Press for supporting this book and its predecessors. First, thanks to Coach Jen Enderlin, our terrific editor, as well as to the brilliant John Sargent, Sally Richardson, Matt Baldacci, Jeanne Marie Hudson, Steve Kleckner, Jeff Dodes, Brian Heller, Jeff Capshew, Michael Storrings, Paul Hochman, John Murphy, John Karle, Caitlin Dareff, Stephanie Davis, Talia Sherer, and Anne Spieth. We appreciate so much your enthusiasm for these books, and we thank you for everything you do to support us. And we will always love and remember the late Matthew Shear, whom we adored.

We'd also like to thank Mary Beth Roche, Laura Wilson, Esther Bochner, Brant Janeway, and St. Martin's audiobook division, especially for giving us the opportunity to record our own audiobook of this volume and the others in the series. We love to do it, and we love audiobooks! And there is simply no substitute for our Philly accents, which come free of charge!

Huge thanks and love to our amazing agents, Molly Friedrich, Lucy Carson, and Nicole Lefebvre of the Friedrich Agency. Thanks to *The Philadelphia Inquirer,* which carries our "Chick Wit" column, and to our editor, the wonderful Sandy Clark.

One of the best people in the world is Laura Leonard, and her advice, friendship, and love sustain us. Laura, thank you so much for all of your great comments on and suggestions for this manuscript. We owe you, forever.

Love to our girlfriends! Lisa would like to thank Nan Daley, Paula Menghetti, and Franca Palumbo, and Francesca would like to thank Rebecca Harrington, Katy Andersen, Courtney Yip, and Megan Amram, and the men she trusts just as much, Ryder Kessler and Nat Osborn. We're blessed in all of you.

Family is the heart of this book, because family is the heart

The Flying Scottolines

of everything. Special thanks and love to Mother Mary and Brother Frank.

We still miss the late Frank Scottoline, though he is with us always.

Finally, thank you to our readers.

Now, you're family.